BALLAD OF KING HENRY VIII AND SIR THOMAS WYATT

With Foreword
by
Ted Hughes

PRISCILLA NAPIER
SHEPHERD'S HOUSE
COLLINGBOURNE DUCIS
MARLBOROUGH
WILTSHIRE, SN8 3DZ
(Mrs T. M. Napier)

ACKNOWLEDGEMENTS

Like everyone embarking on this subject I am greatly indebted to the Public Record Office for use of the Letters and Papers of Henry VIII, and after them, to A. F. Pollard's celebrated work. Much gratitude also to Professor J. J. Scarisbrick for what is now the standard work on the life of Henry VIII. Thanks are also due to John Bowles and Robert Lacey for their enlightening books on the subject; and to all those scholars, known and unknown who studied and translated many invaluable parts of the French Royal Archives, the Spanish, the Imperial at Vienna, the Vatican Archives, and the Venetian Calendar of State Papers.

Many grateful thanks also to Professor Kenneth Muir for his Life and Letters of Sir Thomas Wyatt (Liverpool University Press, 1963); to the Muses' Library Edition of Wyatt's poems, taken from the Blage MS in the Library of Trinity College, Dublin; and to the British Library for the Egerton MS (274) and for the Devonshire MS (Add. MS 36529), for Catherine of Aragon's letter to her husband after Flodden and for Wyatt's letters and those of his father, Sir Henry Wyatt. Most of the obituary verses to Sir Thomas Wyatt are by his Cambridge friend, Sir John Leland, in his *Naenie*. Any others are from Tottel's *Songs and Sonnettes*, or from the Blage MS, and could be by any of his friends—John Poynz, Francis Bryan, George Blage, or John Mason. The generous tribute by Lord Surrey was unquestionably written by him.

Any picture of this epoch must be inadequate; there is so much that we do not know. But anything in inverted commas was actually said or written by whoever's name is alongside in the margin.

FOREWORD

A drama, an epic, a meditation—this poem combines each of these forms on the grand scale.

Priscilla Napier has already, in other books, established her credentials as a scholarly historian. Her long, dramatic verse pageant, ***Plymouth in the War***, which was broadcast on the BBC at the Fiftieth Anniversary of the Plymouth blitz, displayed her skill as a manipulator of a wide range of voices in powerful verse. That same work revealed her peculiar gift for writing dramatic verse that is both freely vernacular and loftily hieratic—the combination invented by Shakespeare. This combination has appeared rarely, in our literature, because few writers have possessed both of the two main requirements.

The first of these requirements is a facility, a knack, for writing pentameter lines that sound simultaneously direct, simple, spontaneous and yet have a ring of inevitability, a moulded finality. The second requirement is a steady, vividly imagined, wide-open, long-range historical perspective, in which all the big issues are assembled and pressing to be heard. There is a third requirement, obviously, which is: the ability to express, and dramatise, the latter through each phrase, each word, of the former. Priscilla Napier brings this off, in a fascinating manner, not just here and there but constantly, throughout: it is simply her natural style of writing, the way her mind works. The whole thing unfolds without any sense of labour or striving for special effects.

Her more personal, lyrical poems reveal a further qualification. Public, objective poetic works depend, finally, for their power to interest us, on a subjective factor. A purely objective work about the Plymouth blitz or Henry VIII would be a prose history. But those short yet massively-structured private poems of hers are moving, almost painful evidence that Priscilla Napier is a deeply subjective writer, and that her poetry, in general, expresses a profound and deeply seasoned emotional private life. The link between the outer twigs and branches and that deeper root, in the larger works, is invisible, but one can feel it, and without any doubt the life of that link is what compels her to write in verse rather than prose. In some real sense, this author has internalised England's history as her own history. Writing about the events and personalities of the one she is inevitably expressing the passions of the other. Each is suffused with the glamour, sorrow, grandeur and drama of the other.

This being so, the actual form of her writing becomes understandable. The pageant-like medley of drama, epic and meditation is not what one would call 'modern' in the sense that book reviewers understand the term. At the same time, it is not archaic or dated. It exists, in its own unique fashion, within a certain sense of 'Englishness'. This 'Englishness' constitutes a living tradition, and a real place, within which Shakespeare's verse, Milton's, Dryden's, Pope's, Wordsworth's and perhaps Owen's, are all contemporary with each other, where all are simply dialects of that state of mind. It is a continuum in which time does not pass but history does accumulate and grow. For all who share this state of mind, the account of the battle of Agincourt and the account of the Battle of Britain stirs us as if they were happening right now, or might happen again tomorrow, with the sure knowledge that we are involved in those actions and cannot be separated from them.

This is not everybody's state of mind, of course. One can easily find gifted young English writers for whom Shakespeare is as alien, as obsolete, as Henry VIII's suits of armour. For Priscilla Napier, as for me, his language is closer, more deeply natural in its essential life, than that of any living writer.

Her poem belongs to and continues to express that state of mind, in the language and poetic form created by that state of mind through England's history. So it is a poem for those who feel, who solidly know, that England's history, in all its details, is somehow their own personal, secret history. As such it seems to me a true work, deeply moving and satisfying.

TED HUGHES, *25th February 1994*

"He is a wonderful man, and has wonderful people round him, but he is an old fox."

Gaspard de Coligny, Sieur de Castillon, French Ambassador in London,
reporting on King Henry VIII in 1538 to King Francis I of France

Hate if you will, but firstly understand
This four square figure astride across the land.

* * * *

"Wyatt the nonparell,
Who Britain's glory showed,
From whose melodious mouth
The well-tuned verses flowed . . . "

A contemporary friend, John Leland

"The ever jesting, never jeering Tom"

Another of the same

Sir Thomas Wyatt by Hans Holbein

The Royal Collection, 1994, by kind permission of Her Majesty the Queen

PART ONE

1

King Henry

The ogre image and the many wives
Are all the reputation that survives.

Repentance is the diet I'll be needing,
Such views imply.

An adept such as I at special pleading
Prefers to justify.

I lived within the ethic of my day
No better, and no worse.
My difference was intensity of purpose;
I held a plan—coherent government—

Reader

Pursued without remorse for human life
Or men's despair, or many a dying curse—

Henry

—Administration fitly organized,
Tempered by Parliament and taught by time
Was carried on by my wise daughter Bess
That brought to many, peace; to few, duress.

Would Francis Drake have sailed around the world
If in the chaos of a weak misrule
His country had been hurled?

Not even my worst enemy supposes
That Shakespeare could have acted or have written
Within the turmoil of the Wars of the Roses.

But this you still forget
Damning me heartily. And yet, and yet
If I was faithful and my purpose clear
Why am I here?

Priest

King Henry not in Hell?
You must be joking
Surely the hottest fires for him are smoking?

Henry

No. Its not hell. For that would be for me
The triumph of lust's terrible consummation—
Total enclosure in an empty room
Alone with Anne Boleyn,
Condemned to an eternal copulation
With her I came to loathe.
If you demand as vengeance on my sin
Continual exit of the urge within,
Almighty, that would certainly be it—

Subject eternally to every fit
Of her unholy and neurotic rages,

Henry

Making sad love
Like desert beasts in cages
Only to stem the flow
Of that wild tongue and all its barbed reproaches;
A mating without freedom, without choice
Wherein no joy encroaches
Where love knows no delight
And tenderness no voice;

An endless and unmeaning repetition
As routine as the striking of a clock—
Long echo of the lust that is perdition. . . .

No, its not hell.
For even a gleam of love
Felt once in life down to the very marrow
Of the most brutal being
Lends, even here, its warmth,
Affords me, from this cavernous dry well
Some hope—a kind of freeing.

Reader

The sparkless eyes look down without remorse
From the bland certainty of that broad face
Above the confident swagger of the stance;
The close mouth signals the determined course.

Can such a soul find grace?

Henry

Here stands the golden boy—
A soldier and an athlete and a lover,
Learned and skilled and tuneful and alive
And husband of the proudest girl in Spain
What could my self-enchantment do but thrive?
How could I be all this, and a charming man
And still rest sane?

You won't believe, in the light of what came after,
But hold your laughter.

Venetian Ambassador

Even that cunning cool Ambassador
From Venice, with no special axe to grind
Nor reason to say any such a thing,
Says Henry is "angelic"; and I speak
To Council, not to any jealous King,
And therefore speak my mind.

Henry

I was no angel, ***that*** was always clear;
But well enough to furnish the idea.

In my beginning was the "gentilnesse"
That Chaucer praised. Even Erasmus noted—

Erasmus

"Something of royalty in his demeanour."

Reader
The courteousness to which
A courtly life gave scope.

Henry
When I was young, I headed every letter
"In Jesus is my hope."
I knelt, I sang, I prayed, I went to masses,
Confessed my sins, believed and trusted God.
Sought by all means to make my service better—

The trouble was, life gave me too much rope.

Priest
Yes, and he hanged himself and rightly so,
And passes now to where the devils go.
Purgatory, is it then? A likely story.
Bearing in mind the saints he sent to glory.
Cry out, the many who rejoiced to hear
His passing bell!
Thinking him wholly cruel, and fitly dead,
And rightly on the bitter path to hell.

Henry
Can you ignore my long accomplishment
Deny to me my clear and clever head?
Lazy sometimes, perhaps,
Leaving the deadly grind of government
To all those eager and industrious chaps.
But inly purposeful, when all is said.

Even the young man's love
I had for Spanish Catharine
That took me by surprise
Had something good within it—
Inspite of your cold eyes.

A young man's love made up of dance and laughter
Flush of the body under velvet clothes,
Love that was unpredictable, unwise,
Of seeing my splendour mirrored in her eyes;
Made up of pleasure, gorgeous pagentry,
Of jewels, banquets, fiery tournaments,
Of striving to excel,
Champion as well as king:
The splash and flow of fountains and of wine,
Life taken on the wing.

A grand concatenation of excitements
Of lusty cheering crowds,
Of sporting, hunting, feasting
Under the spreading trees and bannered tents,
All those bent knees to further our least wishes,
The lute-players at evening, and at last
Our loving's long contents.
The world was then our oyster, to be opened
With hasty trembling fingers, swallowed fast.

Priest

Art not your deeds all weighed?
Do you not stand
Deep in a debt that some day must be paid?

Henry

And long, long after
A hundred years, or more, it seemed to be,
When long forgotten was that season of laughter
Another love arrived.
Love wholly other, gradually born,
A love that reached beyond my lustful being
My power-haunted heart,
A love inseparable from random grief
And sudden seering pain,
Love harboured against evil circumstance
And a harsh world's disdain.
A tender adult love
Meeting my need for calm and absolution,
That strange pure love I felt in her brief lifetime
For sweet and silent Jane.

Oh God! If she had lived, my bluebeard image
Might well have been stillborn.
When first she died I was too stunned for weeping.
For three long days I shut myself away
Too broken even to mourn;
Not eating and not drinking, never sleeping
Fearing to waken to such blank dismay.

How shall we tell? The best of human love
Holds in itself the seeds of its decay.
She died when my delight and lust were strong.
. . . But life is long,
Enchantment ebbs away.
I believe utterly that hers would not.
No matter. For Jane died in childbed fever
And a hard heart grew harder than a stone
More merciless than a wild beast in hunger,
And here I crouch alone
In this eternal solitude to rot . . .

Reader

The sparkless eyes look down
The lips compress.
Who shall abide the terror of that frown?

Henry

There's an old prophecy that men repeat
And I in part believe—a self-fulfilling
Tale that I would begin my reign a lamb
And end it as a lion.
Well, we shall see
How loudly I can roar, how softly bleat.
For all my sense, for all my careful schooling,

Henry

Take it or leave it, I am as I am;
A lamb in loving and a lion in killing,
Made for amour, but even more, for ruling,
A cold intelligence my fires distilling.

2

Sir Thomas Wyatt

Born with a witty tongue
Born with the silver spoon
Of ready mirth,
In fifteen three I saw the light of day,
Allington Castle was my place of birth.

A lucky birth, you'd say,
I'd answer, more or less;
And luckier, by any odds, than some.
A Yorkshireman by breeding,
Young sister, younger brother,
Thoroughly schooled at Cambridge, little needing,
Proud of a long unsullied parentage.
Playing by ear, living by rule of thumb,
And English as they come.

Reader

Yet he was never stranger to distress—
His father, whom he loves, good old Sir Henry
Was kept in cruel duress
By the late King Richard, for his faithfulness
To Henry Tudor, exiled, without power.
Kept in a Scottish prison, often racked,
The strong will of Sir Henry never cracked.

Wyatt

My worthy father,
Said to be saved from starving by a cat
Who brought him pigeons in the icy Tower
Of London town—but can you credit that?

Nine lives, ***I*** had, no less.
But meaning the best, no doubt,
This kindly father paired me off too soon—
Alas for matrimony and its stress!
Elizabeth, the daughter of Lord Cobham
Proved an unlucky guess.

Married too early—seventeen and fifteen—
Having no clue what marriage was about,
She proved a faithless wife
Left me with little Tom and little Bess.
My mother gathered them. I opted out
Into a courtly and untrammelled life.

Reader

Here is the reason why
Men will remember Wyatt a long while yet—
Sent on a mission to the Papal Court
By royal Henry (since he knew Italian
And even French), Wyatt discovered Petrarch,
Brought his works home to England—happy day
That set the English sonnet on its way.

Wyatt

Gold was not plentiful, my talents were—
An ear for music and for poetry.
A love of learning, some desire of fame,
Quickness of wit to drive a landed bargain,
Strong nerves, a sinewy frame,
An aptitude for playing any game
Beyond the usual ones of love and war.
And the most telling lyrics ever sung
Since Greek or Latin poets long before,
Or murmured in the sweet Italian tongue,
Stand in my name.

Reader

Tom Wyatt also wore
A youthful arrogance,
Of yellow hair, and lightness in the dance,
Shown in his bearing—but his wit disarms.

Skilled on the battlefield, at ease in courts,
Apt for the meaningful or subtle glance,
His taste is for excursions and alarms—

Wyatt

No so; you underrate me. At the root
I am a poet, searcher after truth,
Skilled player of the lute.

Reader

I grant you all of that—
Good fellow, good companion—cheerful Wyatt.
A restless Tom, with quite enough of spark
To join the King in jousting, or in riot,
Tennis, or love, or a friendly game of bowls—

Wyatt

Which grows less friendly, when the King discovers
Our rivalry—the once and future lovers
Eyeball to eyeball here, and man to man,
Chasing the lovely Anne.

Often King Henry'd written
"In Jesus is my hope",
Yet he's more prone to sin
Though I am less devout.
We're equally hard-bitten
And house, maybe, an equal devil within.
He simply had more scope.

Wyatt — Loving was now cut short:
The King dismissed me briskly from the Court.

Loyalty is not easy for a man
Who sees his sovereign's eye alight on Anne.

We both are married men. I live apart
And feel more need to exercise my heart.

The King enjoys a good and faithful wife;
What need to trespass on our happy life?

Reader — Loyalty to a king
Is an essential thing
If we would hold the commonwealth together
In fair or dirty weather.
Whether the man be perfect or imperfect
He's all we have.
Under Almighty God,
He is our symbol, our identity,
Our magic mountain, and our sacred tree,
(Difficult things to be.)
He is himself the land, woods, rivers, hills,
The very corn in the field,
He is our sword, our shield,
His absence kills.

Wyatt — This faith my father held to exiled Richmond.
King Richard — "Sir Henry Wyatt", (usurping Richard asked him)
In fourteen eighty-two
"Why art thou such a fool?"
And Richard stood to watch while he was racked.

Limbs stretched beyond endurance
Sir Henry kept to his rule.
"Thou servest but for moonshine over water,
Thy master is a beggarly fugitive",
And Richard offered him reward to yield.
Reader — But Wyatt held allegiance,
And after torture, was allowed to live,
Joining his master upon Boswoth field.
And for his loyalty he found good favour
When Richmond wore the crown as Henry the Seventh.

You could maintain he did some clever guessing,
And judgment more than loyalty won the blessing.

Wyatt — Yet, also, if Anne leaves me, I'll be loyal
To Harry, being my king.
Its a strong instinct. And taken all in all
There's not much future in the other thing.

* * * *

Wyatt

"Once in your grace I know I was
Even as well as now is he,
Though fortune so has turned my case
That I am down and he full high
Yet once I was.

Once I was he that did you please
So well that nothing did I doubt;
And though that now ye think it ease
To take him in and throw me out,
Yet once I was . . .

Once I was he to whom you said
'Welcome my joy, my whole delight!'
And though ye are now well payd
Of me, your own, to claim ye quit
Yet once I was.

Once I was he to whom ye spake
'Have here my heart, it is thine own!'
And though these words ye now forsake
Saying thereof my part is none,
Yet once I was.

Once I was he before rehearsed
And now am he who needs must die;
And tho I die, yet at the least
In your Remembrance let it lie
That once I was."

3

Henry

I looked about, even when young and tender.
Made Duke of York at three years old, I knew
—At Eltham, Greenwich, Richmond—
A native habitat of jewelled splendour.

Danger as well; a deep incessant danger
I recognised when I was six years old
And carried by my mother to the Tower
Whilst a rebellion raged against my father;
Inly absorbing more than I was told,
Peril my playfellow, and death no stranger.

I learned the lesson of the swallowed tears
The guarded, secret face
Of a threatened dynasty with all its fears;
I lived my youth along the edge of strife—

How can you judge, whose safe and pleasant years
Never encounter the sharp edge of life!

Henry — My father kept me closely to my book—
God rest his soul, he made me interested.

Reader — He took to writing, this intelligent prince
To medicine, to wood-carving,
—skills he's forgotten since—
Made poetry, and sang, and played the lute,
Greensleeves composing,
Talked easily in Spanish, Latin, French,
Italian even—every sport contested
Early awake to wrestle or to shoot.

Henry — What would you have, from a Renaissance man?

Reader — Rather more concentration;
Your father's skills of state.

Henry — Surely these things can wait?
Hunting and girls for certain, I enjoyed;
I also read
Thomas Acquinas, loved theology;
Argument spawned and flourished in my head.

Reader — But when his serious father died, ah then!
Henry's enormous passion for enjoyment
Found full employment.

Henry — Posterity has settled me in bed:
Believe me, I was oftener out of it;
Outrageous in vitality, and fit
To ride, to feast, to sing, to dance, to play
Long after dawn came glowing over Windsor
And the wide valley quickened into day—

Tourney and tennis, riding at the ring,
Dangers of hunting, perils at the joust—
After that studious and well-guarded childhood
Everything had a relish and a sting—

Reader — —Everything sped the journey
The royal road to limbo and dismay—

Henry — Who that is young, and well, and had the chance
Would not devour the time with sport and dance
Music and dalliance and long draughts of love?

Reader — But all the while an arid sense of caution
Lived in his mind, and chilled his warmth of heart.
Majesty, with its glories and its perils
Set him apart.

Reader

And so did his diverse inheritance—
Gainst splendid John of Gaunt
And the madness of the Valois King of France
There was his father's family to set—
Those clever, lively, enterprising Welshmen,
Not burdened much with scruple or regret.

Henry

Tudors have always known their way around
And of two pathways, chosen the right fork,
And crossed, lightfootedly, the quaking ground.

Reader

First, Owen married a Princess of France
Widow of conquering Henry, and the second
His son, young Edmund, married Margaret Beaufort,
Grandchild of Famous Gaunt.
Plantagenet echoes rolled through Henry's boyhood,
And this archaic haunt
Of legendary Kings
Was springboard from whence Richmond married England
And with it, young Elizabeth of York.

Henry

So who can challenge? I am in myself
Their son, the true, the undisputed heir—
Who in himself encloses
In one flesh Lancaster and doughty York
The reconciliation of the Roses—

Reader

But subtle enough to take a lot of care
That challengers beware!

Careless enough to waste a lot of money
His canny father carefully put by.

Henry

—Wars of the Roses, whose sharp thorns once tore
My living country nearly to its death
Not all that long before.
I stood, when once my brother Arthur died
Sole, between them and chaos come again
In the long agony of civil war.

How should I not think highly of myself
I who was Norman and Plantagenet,
The passion and the subtlety of Wales
The strength of England's yeomanry and archers,
Master of that persuasion that prevails
And lifelong darling of the English race
The sun and moon, whom sin may not deface?

Sure, I was deaf to clamour and disgrace
To human waste and pain.

Who can resist the devil
When charm is linked to pride
And fate ensures that nothing is denied?

Reader

There's been enough of dangerous calculation
And well-exploited sexual success
Among the Tudors, to leave Henry free
To choose his bride himself;
Since Owen Tudor, with his bold bright eyes
Began the first astonishing enhancement
And married a Princess
To the court's great surprise.
And must inherited ambition lock
So that we tangle with a tainted stock?
Were there not fair and healthy girls at home
In this reverberrant nation?
Why must old Henry go for power again,
Casting his eyes, in vain imagination
Upon the grandeur and the gold of Spain?

Henry

So fated Catharine came, and married Arthur
My elder brother, who was Prince of Wales;
Who boasted on the morrow of his wedding
He had been many furlongs into Spain.
Who now can tell? He was a lively boy

Reader

And fifteen years is deemed a lively age—
Those winter months at Ludlow, in the rain,
When weeping clouds come rolling out of Wales
Day after day, on long Atlantic gales,
Did they not then engage?

Queen Catharine swore they did not, but by then
(Though by Prince Arthur seven times she's bedded,
Poor lady, she was fighting for her marriage
Her throne, her grandeur, her religious faith,
Was ailing, middle-aged, and no more loved.)

Henry

My brother died; but if I knew his carriage
And that of most young men
Their pride, their ardour, lack of hesitation—
Be very sure that there was penetration.

Reader

(Catharine was truthful. But then women dream
And dream untruthfully when left alone.)

Henry

So Arthur died, and our young brother Edmund;
And I was left in perilous isolation
The only male entitled to the throne.

Entitled too, to Catherine it would seem,
The Pope allowed, against the Canon Law.
My father's avarice determined it,
Wanting to keep her dowry of riches,
And truth to tell, I minded not a whit,
Sturdily re-inforced in self esteem
By such a royal bride.

Reader — And soon, his father died.

Henry — Nothing now stood between myself and mine—
The rakehell life, the power and the pride
Just turned nineteen, and flower of all my line.

Even although they hate him—I did not—
Most men will mourn a father newly dead,
The wise experienced guardian, the protector
Surer than all.
But as I rise from kneeling by the pall
And, splendidly apart,
Walk down the aisle after the funeral mass
One thought, one feeling, one emotion sing
In my robust incalculable heart
My calculating head,
Rising above remorse for my shortcomings,
Sorrow or shock or dread—
Knowledge that I am King!

Nobody to control me, none to bid
My come or go, oppose my Yea or Nay!

Where's the nineteen-year-old in glowing health
Who would not do exactly as I did?

4

Henry — Sing Ho! the ocean wave
Where the dark waters lave
Pale cliffs, in all the wildness of my seas!
In a great ship was where I loved to be.
In sailors' coat of freize
Over my cloth of gold and velvet sleeves,
And a large whistle slung around my neck
I'd proudly go to sea.

Happy to pace the deck
Of vessels richly gilt
Regent and ***Sovereign***—these were both my father's—
And Portsmouth Dockyard; all the rest I built—
The ***Henry Grace à Dieu***, called the Great Harry,
The ***Nicholas***, the ***Leonard*** and the ***George***,
Chatham and Deptford Yards, the Channel Forts,
And Woolwich Arsenal. Neighbours to France
Are simple, if they leave defence to chance.

The new yards sounded to the shipwright's hammer—
Harry of Hampton, Mary, Catherine, Anne
Went rocking down the slips,

Henry

And ***Nicholas Montigo*** took the sea,
And ***Mary Rose***, the peerless, the unique,
Finest of all my ships.

Sailors I much esteemed.

Howard,
Lord Admiral

''In Christendom I never saw poor men
In courage to be doing as yours be''
Howard reported, and he thought my vessels
''Gorgeous ships for their burden'', and to him
''The noblest ship of sail'' the ***Sovereign*** seemed.

Henry

Invaders thus prevented,
Our restless genius still was not contented.
For the first time in the long history
Of war at sea
We pierced their wooden sides with ports for guns.

The movement of a great ship under sail
Was joyful to me, and the slap and flurry
Of waves along her side,
The silken softness and the swish of water
Were clean, exciting. And the banners' pride
Rolling above the tide
Moved in me strangely in their ceaseless moving.
And up aloft the shouting and the hurry
Of seamen at the ropes,
The whole taut company of gallant men,
Huge energy of wind, and confident hopes,
Throb of the drum along the morning decks,
The bugles and the fifes
Were music in the heart. And at the launchings
I joined in spirit in the dedication
Of bishops blessing in their gleaming copes.

All this I loved; and with my love was carried
Knowledge of puissance under French attacks,
A sense of triumph and of duty married.

My grandsire, great King Edward
Trounced them at Sluys by sea.
I mean to be adventurous as he.

Reader

After a century such claims grow tenuous.
France is a nation now;
Not a rich pasture helpless under robbers.
Are there not other ways of being strenuous
And winning fame?

Henry

None closer to my heart that I could name;
Except the over-riding need for a son.

Reader

What of the waste of gold?

Henry

Don't think of me un-handsome
Spending it all on jewels and high living!
Often I organized and paid the ransome
Of "Christer prisoners from the infideles",
And later, spent immense monastic wealth
Building this Navy and these naval ports,
Construction yards, and the convenient forts
For guarding them; endowed the guild of pilots,
Trinity House.
And all this preparation
Founded the Fleet that held the dread Armada
Forty years on, thus laying sure foundation
That turned this feudal kingdom to a nation—

How call the money wasted?
Before this vital century was over
No longer dupe of Aragon or Venice
With active ships we held the Straits of Dover.

5

Venetian Ambassador

"Tall of his stature and superbly formed,
Of very handsome presence—" so records
The Venetian Calendar, of this young man
To whom the envoy's heart has clearly warmed.
"And he is past all measure affable;
I never saw a prince more well disposed
Than is this one", he wrote;
"And also he is learned and accomplished . . .
Most generous and kind".

Reader

Ambassadors of Venice's Republic
Having no jealous monarch to report to,
But an impartial Council,
Could be relied upon to speak their mind.

Henry

Though they condemn my looks
Authors should love me better than they do,
For all my life I went on buying books
And reading them, printed or manuscript . . .

Reader

Yet he was frivolous, at play for ever,
At water parties, dalliance, and disguisings,
Or for a wrestle stripped—
Any amusement new.

Henry

King in activity, in dress, in looks,
Calling my dogs, teasing my fools, and yet
Never myself a fool, acute and clever.

Henry

Action! Excitement! Change!
Who'd yawn and stifle in the Council Chamber
When he could ride the range?

The golden boy, beloved of all my people
Athletic, musical, and fair, and strong,
My sign was Loyal Heart, knight-errantry
The burden of my song.
I scattered gold in showers, all along,
As if it were confetti
At every saintly shrine upon my way,
Nothing of my extravagance was petty.
But underneath there was another role
Early begun, increasingly to play—
A steely resolution
For cruel execution
Of Empson, Dudley, Edmund de la Pole.

Equal determination
That just as soon as there was half a chance
I'd follow my inherited obligation
And have a stab at France.

Between whiles, I was happy to dictate,
For instance, over that rough sister Isle,
And here, at first, I was a moderate.

I advocated for the Irish maze
"Politic drafts and amiable persuasions
Founded in law and reason . . .
Practised in sober ways";
Hoping in time to turn
That medieval marsh
That wilderness of chieftains in dispute
And cattle-raiding kern
To more developed life and calmer days.

Mountjoy soon told me different. He was there
As Viceroy, in precarious control
Of this bear garden.
I wanted him to play a better role;
But life's too full and lively to discover
What really makes these gentlemen tick over.
Too soon they seem disruptive beyond pardon
And how find out
For whom the bell in justice ought to toll?

A profitless expanse, a weary zone
Of quaking bog, set round by turbulent sea
Green home of bigotry;
I thought it ever prone
To dangerous attacks of treachery,
Too vulnerable to be left alone.

Henry

And soon I tire of ''aimiable persuasions''
In Ireland; leave my henchmen to dragoon
This luckless and unfathomable country
In all rebellions and on all occasions.

* * * *

Henry

On New Year's Day of fifteen and eleven
        Came a gift straight from Heaven—
Queen Catherine bore to us a living son
Prince Henry, to succeed as Henry the Ninth
        Some distant day!
The red wine flows in ceaseless celebration.
But brief was that fair life so well begun
        He died before the spring.
Why does fate so afflict this faithful nation
        In this defeating way?

        Now for a change of scene
        War is the very thing.
With admirable cause, that doughty fellow
        Pope Julius the Second
Is now at war with contumacious France,
        —It's holy war, agrees the priestly Gown.—
Almost before Louis the Twelfth had reckoned
I landed troops in Gascony, and Spain,
Where Ferdinand, as usual, let us down.

        If France be over-run
Pope Julius offers me a glorious crown
The throne of France itself; with this, the title
        Most Christian King!
Ah, once again we'll own those long lost lands
        Castle and tower and town!
My mighty name through Christendom will ring
        Unto its furthest reaches,
(Whatever good Dean Colet daily preaches.)

Austria, Spain, the Pope, the Netherlands
Are now united, and a match for France
In such grand company I would advance
        On the Imperial side;
And help Pope Julius, and threatened Venice
That holds the Turk at bay; and make a splash
Of military glory, to enhance
All the old triumphs of Plantagenet
At Crecy, Poitiers, and at Agincourt,
And sharpen up my army; and in short
        Would cut a dash
At that old enemy, perfidious France.

Reader

The Council shake their heads, and only Wolsey
    —His faithful almoner—
Provides the guns, stands firmly at his back,
But even he is cautious of the proceedings.

Wolsey

Less than three million subjects to your kingdom
    And you attack?

Henry

Why are some men so dourly down to earth
Seeing each glorious enterprise in black?
Experience has taught how many Frenchmen
One single stubborn Englishman is worth.

Reader

Repulsed at Fuentarrabia, since we fought
True to our normal form, in fierce retreat
Armed with the weapons of the war before,
And ate too much, and, sickened in the heat,
We're back in England, cross but undismayed.

Henry

And I next year, most gorgeously arrayed,
Set forth myself, better equipped, to fight;
Where we accomplished the courageous feat
Of taking Tournai, and defeating France,
And to my huge delight
Capturing even Bayard, peerless knight.

What triumph at the Battle of the Spurs!
    Dancing and song at Lille,
Riding with Maximilian to Tournai—
    What glory tis to feel
And almost grasp, the Lilies for my banner!
    And here's a solid gain
My sister Mary is accepted bride
For Maximilian's grandson, King of Spain;
I preen myself in a right orgulous manner.

I'm called the Emperor's son, the Emperor's brother,
    And swallow all the honey,
Quite unaware he only wants my money
Not my establishment as King of France,
    I glory in my triumph.
Now comes from Scotland news of such another.

Soon as the King of England's back is turned
Our border lands are certain to be burned;
Brother-in-law King James is no exception.
    He is in league with France
    And would be hardly human
    Could he resist this chance.
    So his rumbustious clansmen
Come raiding south to a terrible reception.

Reader

Surrey is waiting for him;
That brave and skilful soldier, who became
The wicked Duke of Norfolk, who could claim
Betrayals by the dozen to his name,
But who behaved superby
This bright September day on the field of Flodden.

Henry

Although forbidden sternly by Pope Julius,
Even so the Scots, at their young chieftain's order
Came roaring over the Border,
Red-bearded, unafraid,
And not to be gainsaid.
Catharine my wife was in the English camp
And when we won at Flodden, felt no pity,
None of a victor's shames
For the defeated Scots
Who fell around King James
In devastating numbers, and felt none
For this brave brother-in-law who died in vain.
She would have claimed his body for a trophy
To send to me in France
But that ''oure englisshmen with tendre hearts''
Prevented her, she wrote, from this fell gesture.
Though small and stout, Queen Catharine wore the vesture
Of callousness, learnt long ago in Spain.

I'm hard enough myself:
But posting fallen kings
Like trophies of the chase,
And one so closely kin to us, displays
Indifference to indignity and pain,
And the great need of reverence to the dead.
Mingled with my old love
And the remembrance of our happier days
There dawned a cold disdain.

Yet preparations for attacking France
Were set in motion, heartened by the fact
That now the Scots were briefly out of action:
And after silencing the Council faction
I went on daily;
And so the deadly dance, the sarabandes,
The to-and-fro of fate, the change of partners,
Brief friendships and the chilly clasp of hands,
Proliferated gaily.

Brandon, my general, was made Duke of Suffolk,
And Howard, admiral, was restored as Norfolk.
Wolsey still aimed for peace
''For the Exchequer's ease . . .
The King's money goeth away in every corner'',

Henry

He wrote of war,
And genuinely hoped the strife would cease.
Since nobody attempts to keep their vows.
He hoped to blaze a trail
As arbiter in European rows.

Nothing of a conclusion is achieved
In this frail league whose holiness grows frailer.
Keen on my reputation as a sailor
We launch attack on Cherbourg on our own.
Despite my raids, my gold,
Our continental allies melt away
And Louis stays secure upon his throne.
Pope Julius dies, Leo makes peace with France,
Old Maximilian proves a man of straw,
And Aragon seems eager to betray.

Reader

Harmony's out of sight
And only the expensive Swiss will fight.
After a year or two of shilly-shally
Good Bishop Richard Fox, the Pope, and Wolsey
Industriously conspire
To bring the kings to truce with one another
And ease their everlasting royal ire.

From Spain the envoy Stiles complained to Henry

Ambassador Stiles

''All policy and craft be here used
More for thayre awne securitie
Than naturall love and kindness to thayre fryndes.
It passes my pore understanding.''

Reader

But Henry understood
His tricky father-in-law of Aragon.
And the King soon was banding
With France, in friendly talk,

Henry

That we should keep Tournai
And a large indemnity,
The King to marry with my sister Mary
As early as might be.
Wolsey, more fortunate,
Became Archbishop of York.

But take it all in all

Reader

This foray into Europe's been a failure—
No real gain at all.
Henry, confronted by the unexpected
Withdrew his men, their tail between their legs,
And lost a lot of wealth,
A lesson that is sure to be neglected.

Henry

The Holy League, no go!
The Emperor's grandson, Charles of Burgundy

Henry

Rudely rebuffed my plans,
Mary, my Princess sister
His promised bride, he summarily rejected.
Is it surprising that I'm disaffected?
Marry, No!

Reader

They do not take King Henry ***au serieux***:
His caracoles across the Continent
Are something for the birds;
An idle dream, his hope to reign in France.

Henry

They chatter so?
Then they shall eat their words.

PART TWO

6

Reader

Treaty with France once signed
Wolsey is full of pride
And Henry satisfied.
His pretty sister joined him in a play,
And banquets and a dance
Hailed her betrothal to the King of France,
Lacking the finer music of romance
Since he is fifty-two, she seventeen,
And called "a nymph from Heaven, a paradise
Most lovely to be seen",
By the Venetian envoy
Moved by her lovely eyes.
Poor pretty Princess Mary, sacrifice
To this unlikely-to-be-lasting peace,
Which signatories mostly fail to keep;
Their brotherhood soon falling fast asleep.

Questions of daughters and of dynasty
My father Henry always bore in mind.
Generally on the make,
But also anxious to secure his frontiers.
Margaret was married to the King of Scotland—

Dunbar

"London thou art the flower of cities all!"

Reader

Dunbar had written, riding in the wake
Of Scottish James who'd come to marry here,
And in a happy hour
To bury the remembrance of sad battles—
Berwick and Bannockburn.

Dunbar

"London, of cities all thou art the flower!"

Reader

Now the young Mary was designed for France
Whose ancient king was withered up and small,
A bridegroom to appal,

Henry

But also our condition to enhance.

Reader

For in this curious matrimonial dance
Princesses are regarded as fair game,
And do regard themselves, or so it seems,
Preferring royal splendour
To any love spontaneous and tender.

Henry

My sister Mary would be just the same,
So I assumed. But Mary disagreed.
Take courage, I assured her; be at ease
Marrying ancient Louis:
He'll kill himself in his attempts to breed.
And then, you're free to marry whom you please.

Reader (With Mary went a small dark English child
With lovely eyes and calculating glance,
Called Anne Boleyn, to be amongst her ladies
On marriage to this ageing King of France.)

Henry Mary had luck; he died.
And Francis, newly king,
And full of oats, made lusty passes at her.
But Mary was a match for anything.
As Queen of France, and as the toast of Paris
Grown confident and grand,
Her Tudor spirit did not hesitate—
Prince Charles of Spain, she said, would be too late—
She'd married handsome Suffolk out of hand.

Reader Happy enough, Suffolk wrote nervously
To Wolsey, fearful of a King irate,

Suffolk "Me nown good Lord, pray . . . help!"

Reader Wolsey advised his lordship to keep calm
And simply concentrate
On keeping Mary's dowry, jewels and plate
Out of the hands of Francis—
Suffolk won;

Suffolk And so a happy marriage was begun.
(Less happy was the day
For granddaughter, Jane Grey)

Henry Thus, in the gamble that we played so hard
All over Europe, at the death of Louis
I lost a valued card.

Francis was steely in a different manner
He loved the pride and pageantry of war
Sound of the trumpet, waving of the banner,
As I did; but, like me, he grudged the money
If not the men, to make this merry hell.
We went on playing poker just the same—
This deadly and incalculable game.

Francis was full of the fighting joys of spring,
A predatory king
And a renaissance man.
He made a gallant dash and took Milan;
Made trouble in the North
Sending to Scotland Regent Albany
With a disruptive plan;
My sister Margaret, the Queen of Scotland
Without her son, was rudely driven forth.
There's little hope that Austria now will rally,
And Richard Pace in Zurich,

Henry

Sent there by Wolsey to recruit the Swiss
And to encourage my collaborator,
Found Maximilian marching on the Brenner
        In all too brief a sally,
Attacking Francis—and then turning back
        A few days later
Having become extremely tired of this.

In England, Henry's queen has had a daughter
Mary, a child who lives. Henry is happy jousting
        And later, with his Queen
Has gone a-maying, dressed in Lincoln green.
While Wolsey, now made Cardinal, decides
Negotiation would not come amiss.

Wolsey

Making a friendship with the King of France
Will not involve us in too great a wrench
        In parting with Tournai.

Maximilian

Says Maximilian to his grandson Charles
        Better to live and fight another day,
"I'll cheat the English, while you cheat the French."

* * * *

Reader

Treaty of London in a while ensues.
"This was the best deed ever done in England"
Good Bishop Fox assured the Cardinal
Who gave a banquet—"richer" people said
"Than Cleopatra, or Caligula".
Everyone felt the treaty was good news.

Eleven kinds of meat, and nine of birds,
Loaded the tables at the Cardinal's dinner,
Salmon, and swans, and fifty-dozen larks,
Butter and cream and frumenty and quinces,
—Nobody gave a thought to getting thinner—
Chickens and marmalade and bright green ginger,
        And every sort of thing.
The baby Mary came in cloth of gold,
Trothed to the Dauphin with a tiny ring.

The Popes had long been urging a crusade,
But powers never held together long.
        Now, an attempt was made,

Henry

A treaty, solemnized at Westminster,
Of almost all the European powers
        Had here a milder aim—
The unity of Christendom at first
        And, this achieved, crusade.

Henry

Everyone signed the treaty, and St Paul's
Resounded to the praise and the acclaim—
Spain, Austria, France, the Pope,
Denmark and Portugal, the fighting Swiss,
(No more to be employed as mercenaries),
Echoed the hope;
And small pugnacious powers in full array—
Venice, Urbino, Guelders;
While England, to complete it, gave Tournai
Back to King Francis,

Reader

(Hardly worth keeping, some said, anyway.)

League of United Nations
Hail the day!
Long live the peace here made!
Wolsey achieves the European grade
(The Pope left very slightly in the shade.)
King Henry swells with pride
Feeling himself a general benefactor
And world-stage actor.

Meanwhile the stubborn English population
Who'd missed out on the party
And felt that all the fountains spouting wine
Were rather less than hearty,
Could see no cause for this peace celebration.

Suddenly, on the Evil First of May
This fifteen seventeen
The populace of our aggressive nation

Citizen

Decide against appeasement, and set fire
To London embassies, and merchandise
Of foreigners in store.
Merchants and craftsmen, coming from abroad
Here let them trade no more!
They hurtled insults at ambassadors,
Threaten the Mayor, Wolsey, the Corporation.

Reader

These floutings of the law
Arouse King Henry's wrath and indignation,
The ring-leaders are hung and drawn and quartered,
The rest for mercy plead;
And the King's rage is only to appease
By good Queen Catharine kneeling on her knees.

Henry

She still is my good angel;
Although her father, Ferdinand of Aragon
Has double-crossed me thrice
And I desire revenge,
Kate is still wifely, kindly, truly nice,
Intelligent and handsome,
A true domestic paragon.

* * * *

Henry

The London rebels quieted,
With very small persuasion
In celebration of this truce with Francis
We planned a party to make glad the occasion,
Setting a sumptuous scene.
Five thousand English carried across the Channel
To those (still English) lands
Round Calais and round Guines.

The Field of Cloth of Gold! the horses neighing
Three thousand of them mine, a great pavilion
Made out of wood and glass—

Reader

A leather case, Our Lady's form conveying
Among the serried and flamboyant tents,
Fluttering pennants, and the smell of grass
Trodden of many feet
As rainbow-vested courtiers bend and pass . . .
Wolsey in full control,
Sir Edward Watson, the wide scene arraying—
The quails, the sturgeon, and the Hypocras;

Henry

The beat of drum, the woodwind, and the brass
Shouting their music, stimulant and sweet,
The noise of joust, vaingloriously displaying,
Swirl of rich garments, and the glow of gold,
Sparkle of jewels, and the routine praying . . .
The warm smell of hot horses; in the tents
Cloth-of-gold boys, who most delicious scents
Through the close air continually kept spraying.

We sparred, as each proud monarch circumvents
His rival, tries to keep the other sweet,
Yet can't resist the challenge to out-run
And bring the other peacock to defeat.

Wolsey

What flaunt, what folly on this field of Guynes!
This would have built a college three times over
And left his soul in clover . . .

Henry

So thought the sobersides. They should have seen
The cloth of gold caught in the summer sun,
The floating of brave banners,
The wine, the food, the feating and the fun,
All the urbane extravagance of manners—
Ah yes! They should have seen
That broad sweet valley under the summer sun
My land of Guines;
The flash of level lances
The flash of eyes that signal through the dances
And signal not in vain;

Henry

The halberdiers, the hawking, and the hounds,
And the outlandish sounds
Where lesser revellers, all about the plain
Try, laughingly, to understand each other.

And from either country
Of these long-lasting, age-old enemies,
Came two great parcels of nobility,
With old crusading names—
Brave Knights, and lovely ladies, good as gold:
And doubtless just as many
Brash fellows, flighty dames,
And all superbly gowned;
And in the lucky blaze of summer weather
Jousting and wrestling, frolicking together,
Then in a burst of music
Sweet and holy,
Two royal choirs sing in harmony
Across the Val d'Or ground.

And everywhere, the gold!
Francis of France and I
Waltzed round each other as two wary wrestlers
Seeking a hold.

This pride of France
(Whose triumph soon, in Italy, would be
Anathema to me),
Bore a hook nose, slanting deceptive glance,
Great eyes he had, but poor and spindly shanks,
He had the expertise, I had the weight:
Wrestling, he threw me; and they parted us
By anxious partizans securely held
Before I could in wrath retaliate;
But in the field of jousting ***I*** excelled.

Francis

The Field of Cloth of Gold—and two shrewd fellows
Under the velvet hats and ostrich plumes,
Behind the jewels and the silks, aware
Of having and not having
What had once been and might again be there,
Of Normandy, Poitou, and Aquitaine.

Henry

He had the richer nation
And five times England's sturdy population.
Both had enormous appetite for pleasure.
We both were tall, he had the suppleness,
I had the looks, the ruddiness, the presence,
We both had pride, and careful calculation;
Clever and keen, taking each other's measure,
With equal aptitude for spending treasure.

Francis — Two men of the Renaissance, hot and cool,
And no man's fool
However much we're played upon by women.

Henry — And as for France, I had a better claim
As king of this fair land
Than any Valois out of Angouleme.

Through both displayed a genius for enjoyment
I'd more variety in my employment;
We shared a leavening of common sense
A sometimes level head.
I had the confidence.
He had the sons.
A paltry looking bunch, but there were three.
And all my three either stillborn or dead.

Reader — Two ***faux bonhommes***, smiling and cruel and bland
Taking each other warmly by the hand,
Kissing each other as a "Cousin King":
And, slung among the furred and velvet coats
Two thickly jewelled swords
Ready to swing.

7

Henry — Twice over, Maximilian, Emperor,
(And volatile as any weather-cock),
Had offered to adopt me as his heir
Making me King of Rome.
But I was shrewd enough
To know that this affair
Was evanescent as the ocean foam
That the wild sea-winds blow;
Cautiously, I said, No;
Aware that loads of money were involved.

In January of the year nineteen
The Emperor died; his Empire's up for grabs,
(Or, to be more exact, is up for bribes
To the Electors.) Now that I have seen
Francis and Charles are also candidates
My buoyant and competing heart dilates—
How would it be to rule those diverse tribes!

The Netherlands, Burgundians, Milanese,
As well as Germans and the Austrians.
I ride a high, unrealistic hope
I should be Emperor, and Wolsey Pope.

No dice. We lack persistence, and the cash,
And live too far away.

Henry

Nothing can come of it; and Charles is made.
        Our bribes were far too small,
        We came too late in the day,
And took the field with insufficient dash
As if we did not really want to win.
        So Charles is in;
Immensely powerful and distinctly shrewd.
(But Francis anyway is in the shade.)

* * * *

Henry

The grass had hardly grown again at Guines
Before the bubble of this friendship burst.
The fountains pouring claret and white wine
        Had barely ceased to flow
When Wolsey, summing up my new-found friend
Was hard at work, treating behind the scene
        For friendship with the Emperor
Whom yet again I met, at Gravelines.
So soon is polity obliged to go
A miry way that never can be clean.

Good came from these palavers all the same.
As Charles and Francis will not long agree
        England shall arbitrate
        Her king thus growing great,
And this was Wolsey's admirable plea.
This for a while was seen to be
        Glory enough for me.

I'd made a friendship with the King of France
        Which I did not betray
Despite the many blandishments of Spain.
''Henry of England, notable peace-maker'',
        I will be friend of both
        Although I'm nothing loath
To take the field against the first peace-breaker.

''Peaceable ways, without hostility'',
So went the word, to both of them, from me,
Speaking from a sincerity of heart
Not with a tricky diplomatic art,
        Not yet the slave of enmity
        Nor captive of suspicion.
And the peace lasted full three happy years.

* * * *

Henry

This did not check a strong determination
        Seemingly wise to me
        To be secure by sea;
        Caution and passion blended:

Reader

Constructing for this purpose, ships of might
The lilies of their certainty unfurled . . .
And nothing really happens as intended,
Although the vessels, when the bright dream was ended,
Sufficed in conquering, by mistake, the world.

Henry

I loved my valiant darlings of the seas,
Especially those two
The ***Mary Rose***, the ***Henry Grace à Dieu***,
From Portsmouth harbour and from Orwell mouth,
Dodging the currents and the dangerous tides,
Sales crowded for the South.
High as cathedrals, with as many windows
Gold-painted, and gold-wreathed.
Their gun-ports spilling fire and heavy shot,
Their flags and pennants curling,
Rising and dipping, using every breeze,
With many well-armed men to man the lot.

Like great Leviathans, the ocean whales,
They seem to leap the seas,
Ships painted as a harlot, and as proud
As Cardinals afloat in billowing red
Puffed with the puissance of their swelling sails.
Men at the tiller, men at the masthead
Clever as monkeys, and alert as birds . . .
Saint George's English ships
Against whom never a foreigner prevails.

Reader

A doughty sailor king, he thought himself.
So did some others now, soon brought to book.
An outline formidable, never faint.
How did he look?
Holbein has told immortally in paint.

Holbein

High forehead, a nobility of brow
And strength of face, under a reddish thatch;
A tall and square athletic frame to match—

Henry

The body that I used with so much zest . . .
How I once gloried in my strength of arm
And certainly of aim!
And sweet it was for me, as for another
To hear the mounting music of acclaim
The warm full-hearted cheering!
For the rest—

Holbein

The eyebrows arched, a rufus bird in flight,
Narrow determined eyes that don't bely
A small, decided, not un-handsome mouth
With full and sensual lips, quick to deny—

Henry

To sing, to chide, to laugh without restraint,
Ready enough both to command and kiss;
Harry the king of confidence, the last
Of all those super-charged Plantagenets
Whose blood I strongly own, whose power surpassed . . .

Holbein

Fuzz of red beard, not totally concealing
A strong and resolute chin; and all of this
The clothes of jewelled magnificence he wore
Were carried with a confident panache
That bordered arrogance and often passed it—
A mighty sense of majesty revealing.

Henry

"By the Lord Harry!" men would sometimes swear
When I was in my grave four hundred years;
No matter if they thought me better there.

Yes, he could paint, that small industrious Dutchman.
Yet there's a kind of scorn in his depiction,
As if those clever eyes, that subtle brush
Wouldn't discern the truth behind the fiction;
Under the bluff "Hail fellow, and well met"
Never observed a brain as complex yet—

A clever, balancing, observant wit
That never let its purpose out of sight.
        If Holbein guessed at it
And understood the sense beneath the lewdness,
He never knew my longing for creation
Or dreamt that my appearance did not fit
With a mild talent to compose and write;
Though he portrayed a kind of saving shrewdness
Below my readiness to bark and bite.

So stood I, and so was I, to a point.
The holy oil that trickles to anoint
The broad brow of a king, can also hide
The steely mind, or the warm heart inside.

For this same strutting chanticleer it was
        Who knew that England's peace
        Her safety and her strength
Was centred in the power of her ships.
        Those merciless set lips
        Ordered and supervised
Their building and their manning and their guns
        And all their great increase;
        Who multiplied her sailors,
        Joked as a cheerful fellow,
And made them laugh, in echo of that bellow
In which my huge enjoyment found release.

* * * *

Henry

My rich, efficient Minister plods on.
Wolsey was full of labour, night and day.
And to and fro he busied the long hours
Trying to keep the peace between the Kings
        And doing so, for years.
I let him take the trouble of the realm
The while I hunted and enjoyed the ladies,
And splendidly he managed at the helm.

Wolsey

I long for stable government, for peace
        And absence of commotion;
Yet can't resist pulling the strings of power
Towards my own and ultimate promotion.

Henry

But I was no man's puppet, no man's fool.
"Henry the King now pleasured is to hear"
Of justice, and the whole state of the realm
"How idle men be put to occupation",
Frontiers maintained and ably fortified,
Goods put to profit, fighting ships secured
In land-encircled, easy anchorages,
The safety of my dynasty assured.

(Yet what is this, without the needful son
        To take it all in hand?
Sad Catherine has now lost another one.)

* * * *

Reader

Like Thomas More, Erasmus had long hated
The riches and the hard hearts of the priests,
Callous to poverty that separated
        The poor from all life's feasts.

Erasmus

        "Oh tongueless theologians
        Oh dumb bishops
Who in a silent impotence behold
Our endless human miseries unfold!"

Reader

So wrote Erasmus, now a don at Oxford;
Henry followed suit,
Though, with a milder eye on the injustice,
                He directed
        A piercing beam on the loot.

More's great ***Utopia*** was a radical book
In condemnation of mankind's distress.
In other ways he was traditional
Giving new notions an unfriendly look;
        Like Henry, he believed
        In burning heretics,
And in this matter, this delightful man
Was readier to punish than to bless.

Reader

For since the re-discovery
Of Plato, Cicero and Aristotle,
Many too many genies,
Came leaping out of the bottle.

Henry

I followed closely in the Church's teaching.
Though I was learned, and read the humanists
Arguing often "with unruffled temper"
Amongst my bright contemporaries, still
I hated heresy, and unrelenting
Would butcher luckless heretics at will.

For all my love of the Lord
This thought will yet intrude—
Why should the Church own a good third of England
And send the wealth of it so far abroad
To an ungrateful, all-demanding Rome?

I would reform the Church, never deny her:
Flouted authority comes too near home.

Yearly the Church grows more concerned with money
Daily men grow more restless and more rash
Germany seethes already with new learning,
And others, too, for fresh insights were yearning.
An Augustinian friar applies the flash—
In fifteen-seventeen, when Martin Luther
Nailed a great thesis to the Castle church
At Wittenburg, against Indulgencies,
(Papal forgiveness bought for ready cash.)

Luther proclaimed that we are saved by Grace
And justified by Faith;
Not, as in bank accounts, acquiring merit
By piling capital of virtuous deeds
Do we at length the Kingdom of God inherit.

Needing no priestly intermediary
Between ourselves and God,
But needing the immediacy of Christ
And his examplary deeds
And his immortal words;
The individual conscience
Utters more surely than the best of creeds.

Wider than Germany,
All over Europe
Fell Martin Luther's spiritual seeds.

Henry

In 1521 my book was printed
(The first of English kings to write a book
Since Great King Alfred in the far eight hundreds)

Henry

A diatribe against this Martin Luther,
Believing every syllable I penned,
Defending all the Seven Sacraments,
Roundly declared in my ***Assertio***
That Martin Luther erred—
"A puny friar, an insubstantial wraith"
I called him, "A dilapidated weed",
(Never at loss for the compelling word.)

Even my gentle friend, the good Erasmus,
Who hated wars like death,
Was drawn into this fray
Against his will; whilst a delighted Pope
Honoured me as "Defender of the Faith".

A name resounding and magnificent
As were the titles borne by other thrones—
"Most Christian King" of France, "Most Catholic
Of Spain", and "Holy Roman Emperor"
Of Austria, the herald loud intones.
Defender of the Faith. Well satisfied,
In this, as in all else, I always tried
To keep abreast of Jones.

* * * *

Reader

Often as kings would boast of a crusade
They rarely co-incided in desire;
And Maximilian in his grandiose schemes
Widened the field of fire;
His planning to enlist the Shah of Persia,
The King of Georgia, Ethiop Emperor,
In this campaign
Seemed, even to contemporary monarchs,
Almost insane.

Henry

In fifteen eighteen, in my complex being
I'd struck a nobler vein.

Promising to the Pope
So to do battle with the Infidel
As to deny his European hope,
With twenty thousand soldiers
Furnished with guns and other war machines,
I promised his as well
Seventy ships, with fifteen thousand soldiers
All trained to fight at sea,
And full of ardour and fidelity
To send Islamic conquerors to hell.

"If Heaven bless me with an heir before
The sailing day, I'll head the host myself",
I told Pope Leo.

Henry

I looked for some great triumph of the Faith
To Christ's eternal glory;
Clearly could see myself
Ranging romantic forests of the east,
Riding in triumph to Jerusalem
Setting once more the holy places free
As in some ancient story
Of old Crusader lore,
I'd hold at length the gorgeous east in fee.

In bright imagination
I see myself beloved of the Pope,
Like the remembered paladin
Who won three rounds with Sultan Saladin,
I'm Coeur de Lion storming the walls of Acre
And charging at Arsuf,
Edward the First on his black horse Ferraunt
The greatest knight in Christendom; (and also
A young man on a fascinating jaunt
Footloose, aloof,
Escaping from the duller chores of home.)

Nor was this hope all worldly;
I longed my toiling spirit to renew,
In this hard trek and worldly abstinence
Some early inner purity regain,
Dipping my soul into this heady brew.

But this most generous offer
Leo the Tenth decided to ignore,
Though he had earlier urged us on crusade
His present business crowded out the rest—
Turmoils in France and Italy galore,
Whose settlement seemed best.

Reader

And in this way was made
An easy entrance into Christendom.
For all too soon
Ebullient Turks came racing into the west
Under green banners with their crescent moon,
Swarming from out their conquered Istanbul
With undiminished zest.
Their cup of triumph full,
They ravaged through Belgrade and Buda Pest,
Hungary bleeding under savage war,
While Christians fought each other all the more.

Henry

No prospect for Crusade, and we then planned
An expedition through the North West Passage
To find that fabled land
Miraculous but credible Cathay,

Henry

Planting the cross of Christ on a far strand
(And picking up the profits on the way.)
But Cabot, now in Venice, would not play
He'd other fish to fry.
One of our ships was lost, two went astray,
And when at last Cabot applied to go
Occasion had gone by.

Thwarted in doing something good, I turned
Not without relish, to attempting bad.

Spoiled of a far ambition
I turned again to Continental war—
The sure road to perdition.

8

Reader

After the years of peace
War plans were made anew.

Dorset

"Our sovereign Lord is utterly determined
To take his viage into the partes of France"

Henry

Wrote Thomas Grey, Lord Dorset, as I gathered
Forces for war, in fifteen twenty-two.

I was too self-engrossed, too hot to hear
Counsels of caution, uttered sure and clear
By Wolsey, and too confident to fear
Above the maddened beating of the drum
Woe that must surely come—

Reader

The groaning of the wounded, the wild cry
And broken gasp of those about to die.
Too stony hard of heart
Against the starveling child, the lonely tear
Of wife and mother; he was unconcerned
To know the wrack of warfare, win or lose,
The farm and village burned,
The dearth and misery of year on year.

Henry

What are these pains to me?
Such things have always been, must always be

Reader

When the same madness roars across the brain
Till the blood blinds the eyes and burns the heart
And war is made again—Oh God defend us!
And war is made again.

Henry

Francis and Charles, for all their calculation,
In war were just as callous and well-sinewed,
As passionate, as past consideration.

Reader

So on and on, this dance of death continued.

* * * *

Henry

Although not spoiling for a further battle
The throne of France was always my objective
To which descent from my great-grandmother
French Princess Catherine, gave as good a right
As any Valois cousin you could name.

Wolsey

Nor is this sole directive.
Plantagenet descent enforces claim
To Gascony, Guienne, and Normandy,
To pleasant Maine, and hardly won Poitou,
To fair and rivered lands about Anjou.

Henry

Crowning at Rheims must be my destiny,
And the return of all great Henry won
    (Although his time was short)
On the triumphant field of Agincourt.

Wolsey

Francis is now hell-bent for Italy,
And making sudden sallies on his frontiers.

Henry

Here's an aggression every man can see!
(Besides, it wouldn't do to let his skill
Go to his head, and lead to other ventures.
And surely here, the Council will agree.)

Another league is formed. The challenge rings!
Invading France has always been a pleasure
Like hunting, that engages English Kings.

So now, what need to wait?
Here is occasion to fulfil my dreams!
The Emperor agrees. The chance is great.
For Rheims we ride! For Rheims!

* * * *

Henry

Before I leave, necessity dictates
The certainty of safety in my rear.
I still have no male heir, and Buckingham
A powerful Plantagenet, spells danger.
    Outwardly, he placates,

Buckingham

But sometimes can't resist testing the chance
Of royal prospects, with my intimates,
A dangerous toe stuck into perilous water.

Henry

    Before we leave for France
These are suborned. Though, maybe, in the clear
    The poor Duke sweats with fear.
Wolsey with usual cunning has him framed.
    The deadly axe is whirled
The mighty Duke beheaded without mercy,
A powerful subject permanently tamed.

Buckingham
"I went up river as a mighty Duke"
Buckingham mourned, "and down as Edward Bohun
Most caitiff of the world".

Henry
His unexpected end at least came soon.
Now he's despatched
England again with the old foe is matched.

Reader
The march through Picardy
However ***déjà vu***
To the protagonists looks ever new.
Kings are forever hopeful of success
No matter that the last war was concluded
In muddle and in mess,
And for the many kin, in deep distress.

Englishmen sail from Dover;
Meetings at Bruges, attacks towards Compiègne
Are set up once again;
Again are set a-roll
Burgundian drums. Offencives in Provence
Possess the soul.
King Francis moves from Lyons to Avignon;
The Emperor counter-moves;
And then, quite suddenly, the whole thing's over.

Henry
Now is my hour!
Now is it all to win.
I've backed the Emperor through thick and thin,
Lent him a fortune, promised him my daughter,
And I have spared no toils
To entertain him on his way to Spain,
Supplied my troops to help him in the slaughter.
Francis is captured by him,
With two of his young sons.
Let us divide the spoils!

Yet now Charles makes it cavernously plain—
For all my gold
For all my intervention
He never had the most remote intention
That my fantastic project should succeed.
In this harsh moment the long dream is past;
I realize at last
That never shall the crown of France at Rheims
Be mine indeed.

* * * *

Wolsey
Alas for all these high fantastic hopes!
These ancient, long-believed dynastic dreams!

Reader

We simple English never know the ropes
Of European strategy and schemes,
We never fathom Emperors or Popes,
Or the old subtleties of Rome or Greece.
Fog settles in our brains as on our hills,
We win the wars but always lose the peace.

Something in all that innocent salt water
That heaves between the mainland and our shore
Conceals from us the obligatory slaughter
The expense of spirit and the waste of life
Not to say cash, in continental war.
We were the dupes, supplying money-bags
And now the whole conception is in rags.

Henry

And Wolsey, at the helm
Subject to "muttering throughout the realm".

Looked at aloofly, you could say I've learned
The toughness of the Continental problem
Without my fingers being deeply burned;
But not enough to sober me for long.
And also how to make polarity
Between myself and luckless ministers;
That gentle knack of how to put the blame
Where it does not belong.

So, was I wrong?
Wolsey must take the guilt;
Did he not back me to the very hilt?

So joyfully do men set out to conquer
As I to conquer France
Locked in a dream of right . . .
Some ancient and undoubted provenance.
And then discover its a dream indeed,
Lost with the morning light.

Reader

The Emperor Charles has had enough of Henry,
From whom, at last, he can get no more gold.
Henry's great plan for Europe leaves him cold;
He now has Francis where he really wants him
Imprisoned and controlled.
He turns from England, treats King Henery ill,
And marries Isabel of Portugal
Rich with the wealth of Indies and Brazil.

Turning away his supercilious brow
Charles plans to fight the Turks in Africa
With an expression holier-than-thou.

Reader
The Emperor's icy stare
Leaves Henry much affronted
And Catherine in despair.
Her nephew has repudiated wholly
Her darling daughter and her only heir
(The Princess Mary, who's still only nine)
Hope of the English line;
And Henry's aspirations rudely shunted.

Henry
My attitude to Pope and Emperor hardens
And towards blameless Catharine.
The devil take the Hapsburgs!
I make my bastard son the Duke of Richmond
Load him with honours as my possible heir,
And will now cultivate my other gardens.

Honour and glory—
Loved beyond compare!
Nobody goes unpunished
Who jockeys me out of my proper share.

To my ambassador at Charles' court—
"So long" I told him "as the realm of France
All in the heart and midst of Christendome
Situate" . . . Is ruled by those who never will
Content them with enough, but ever still
"Their limits and dominions ampliate",
There never can, nor ever will be quiet.

Wolsey
(No matter if this tendency to riot
In other people's countries at our leisure
Applies to him as well.)

Charles
The Emperor is not impressed. His pleasure
Is to confine himself to things at home
And new-wed Isabel.

Henry
Such an occasion missed!
With Francis in his hands; why can't he see it?
We could have simply occupied French lands,
And I, like Henry Lancaster, be crowned.
Well, if he won't—so be it.

* * * *

Reader
Henry was right about the ceaseless wish
Of France, to "ampliate"
Their wide dominions. Under many a Louis,
And spurred on by Napoleon the great,
The French this tendency would demonstrate.

Reader

England had learned a lesson, and would rather
Stretch her limbs farther.

*　*　*　*

Henry

London can show the graciousness of peace.
Here's the enormous Palace of Whitehall
Like a brick college—courtyard, hall and tower,
Knights out of armour, ladies in a bower,
And taut at anchor on the running tide
Of lovely Thames, my royal barges ride—
Of every city, London is the flower.

Dunbar

"Sovereign of cities, seemliest in might
Of high renoun, riches and royaltie . . . "

Henry

So seemed she to Dunbar, the Scottish poet,
And so she seems to me.
His words resound in my delighted mind.
Is it amazing that I swelled with pride
Playing a tune to which the world might dance
And all my loving commons pleasure find?
When Kings of Spain, of Scotland, and of France
And Emperor himself, walking in line,
Were pleased to wear my Order of the Garter.

The power and glory, like a heady wine
My careful sense defied.

Yet if I cannot leave a son behind
Settled and sure, established on the throne
To all this varied splendour I am blind.

A Spanish girl too quickly loses beauty;
And when that goes, I can't be reconciled.
Catharine was earnest to perform her duty
And now for yet another stillborn child
Another bitter loss, she weeps apart.
Her charity's enormous, she endows
Church after church, abounds in prayers and vows . . .

So many hopes forlornly she has nursed,
Her sad grey eyes are piteous to behold
Her fair brown hair is losing all its lustre—
I see with terror that she's growing old
And why should this our marriage be accurst?
I have brought peace, I've brought prosperity
Then have the saints no charity?
Has civil peace no graces?

Reader

In England now, the streams that ran with blood
Are crystal clear above their beds of gravel,
Between their mimulus aisles.

Reader

The long green hair of water-crowfoot traces
Pure currents, with flotillas of white flowers;
        The forest ways unravel
        No ambush or assault,
And where the tramping armies used to travel
        Our trodden landing places
        No keel of Frenchman scours;
A summer ocean now serenely smiles.

The scarlet battlefield is long since shorn
Of fallen men, and now the happy larks
Flutter above the green forgiving corn.

Is all the butchery, the bitter pain
Of civil war, only to come again
Since the unquestioned heir is not yet born?

Henry

Passion and common sense,
Love for a woman, forethought for my realm
        Will fuse in one desire,
        Will utter with one voice,
And bring me to irrevocable choice.

9

Reader

In early spring of fifteen twenty-six
Wyatt was sent on mission to Cognac
        Under Sir Thomas Cheney
To greet the King of France on his release.
Cheney reports the young man's power to please—
"He hath as much of wit to mark
And to remember, everything he sees
As any a young man in England hath".
With foreigners Wyatt found himself at ease,
        And next year, would embark
        For Rome with Russell.
        Sent by him to Venice
Wyatt was captured by some Spanish troops
        On his way back.
Unlikely to survive, he made escape,
Luckily leaving Rome before the sack
Of the holy city, that most savage deed
        Of Emperor Charles's ***landesknechts***.
He brought back stories that delighted Henry
About some cardinal who could not read.

        For Thomas Wyatt, young envoy,
Was this the first encounter with the sonnet
And with Italian verse in general
Dante and Petrarch, lyric poetry?

Reader — The bright young man, returning slowly home
Turning it in his head and dwelling on it?

* * * *

Wyatt — To the Queen's Majesty—Sir Thomas Wyatt
At her command has "made into oure englysshe"
Petrarch's discourse—***The Remedy of ill-fortune***,
And the same poet's ***Quietness of Mind***;
And to this text now turning

(Not without fault, as those of perfect learning)
Hopes that the Queen will find
Pleasure therein, and cheer
"For the good lucke of this newe yere".

Petrarch — "In long lamenting, sourness of mind,
Leading a dolorous life, we do deny
That goodness of which God himself is author
To us—the natural grounding
Of humankind.

So grieving, we make sorrowful, and defile
Joy that was ours erstwhile.

If we give heed, with clear and open ears
To friends who counsel, and to music sounding,
Hear the sweet song of birds; if we should see
The happiness of beasts that play and dance,
Yet not accept that these dear things can turn,
And thus default on the delights they earn,
How can we come to quietness, or face death?
Or in such change, let be
Some liberty and space to take our breath?

Use the things present as they daily come
Without sad blame;
Rest in the pleased remembrance of things past;
And in God's holy name
Unfearfully, and most assuredly
With a glad shinning hope, at the long last
Draw towards things to come.

Wyatt — (Alas, poor lady, she'll have need of this
And need of every comfort poets offer,
Travelled so far from comfort, and from love's bliss).

Petrarch — "God in his daring leads, himself, the dance
And we should follow him.
Dishonour not, nor do contaminate,
Nor your own life profane

Petrarch

With wailing and with groaning for those things
That cannot come again.
Troubled affections and most tangled business
—Eyes weeping, and teeth grinding—
Afford no solace to the weary brain.
Sorrow must have a term
Grief not forever last.
Receive the present day without fault-finding
Give thanks for joy thats past."

Wyatt

(Alas, Queen Catherine, if you could do so
A kind of life might grow;
Different indeed 'twill be, most sadly other,
Sceptred no more, yet life of a true kind.
Ah do not, as a women set aside,
Into a half-world glide—
Grief your companion and your foster-brother.

Listen to Petrarch, who could surely see
How grievous and destroying loss can be.)

But as for me
My life is lit with a different blaze of weather.
Happily, madly, probably at peril,
I hunt a bird of quite another feather,
The dark-eyed charmer who's appeared from France
With sweet melodious voice and ready wit—
Yes, this is it!
A lady worth the winning, worth the dance.

Anne Boleyn

New come to Court, I need a forceful friend
Yet one whose lusty purpose I can bend,
Affection I can use
To suit a grander end.

Wyatt

"Madam, withouten many words
Once I am sure ye will or no
And if you will, then leave your bourds
And use your wit, and shew it so;

And with a beck ye shall me call.
And if of one that burneth away
Ye would have any pity at all
Answer him fair with yea or nay.

If it be yea, I shall be fain;
If it be nay, friends as before;
Ye shall another man obtain
And I mine own and yours no more."

Anne Boleyn

Here is a love robust, uncomplicated,
By a strong lust dictated,
And, I much hope, un-clinging.

Anne Boleyn

Here is the gallant and attractive man
        Whose praises all are singing,
One who would kiss and never tell,
Ready intelligence, fine voice, the lot—
        One who does all things well.

Here's the brave step in the evening courtyard ringing.
        Arms' length, for a short spell—
        And then, why ever not?

* * * *

Henry

For Catharine, well-desired,
The haute princess from Spain—
Slowly my passion sours.
Now wearily I come to my devoirs
Making a kind of love—
But she's too godly ever to complain.

She still loves hawking. But her mind seems set
In solemn Spanish mien,
Anchored in some lagoon of quiet retreat,
Or trapped in some dim melancholy mesh
Of saints and stillbirths and long sacraments . . .
I needed merriment as men need meat,
To laugh, to act, be merry! How I loved
The world, the devil, and the darling flesh!

I loved her, vaguely, through those twenty years
But tired of those inevitable tears
Flowing, it seemed, from an exhaustless fount
For all those many babies we have lost . . .
Sometimes, I felt, she mortified herself
Just to condemn the spirits that would mount
In my resilient heart.

Am I not King, ever to be obeyed?
Amusement must be made!

Has no man ever tired
Of an old wife grown chilly, anxious, greyed,
Her love the desperate clinging of a vine
No fit response to mine,
Her body weary and her warmth expired?

Reader

Rarely do people consciously exclaim
"Evil, be thou my good!"
                But the ill deed
Once done, enjoys a being of its own,
Once done and unrepented, soon is grown
Into a driving force, alive within,
A tyranny no-one on earth can tame.

* * * *

Wyatt

Now my untroubled love for dark-haired Anne
Begins to be undone.

"And wilt thou leave me thus?
That hath loved thee so long
In wealth and woe among?
And is thy heart so strong
As for to leave me thus?
Say nay, say nay!

And wilt thou leave me thus,
That hath given thee my heart
Never for to depart
Neither for pain nor smart
And wilt thou leave me thus
Say nay, say nay! . . . "

. . . Whom speak I to,
Unkind and deaf of ear?
Alas, lo, I go
And wot not where . . .

Light in the wind
Doth flee all my delight,
Where truth and faithful mind
Are put to flight . . .

Henry

Men call me heartless, venal, and unjust,
Cruel in desertion, wicked in my plan
To wed with Anne.

Let them acquaint themselves with that chill race
That comes from Ferdinand and Isabella
Kings of Castile and Kings of Aragon,
Deeply convinced of an unbounded grace,
A stock profoundly bad;
Degenerate as they are arrogant
With all the bigot narrowness of Spain
Cruel and obsessed and mad.

They may have sent that tireless Genoese
To find the far Cathay,
He found beyond the overwhelming seas
Only some islands manned by cannibals!
These Kings have driven Moors and Jews away
Cleverest of men; and if they would not go,
Made them convert to their dark view of Christ
Or lose the light of day.

Is this the stock from which to breed an heir
To England's stalwart and determined glory?

Henry

There's Catharine's sister—morbid and insane
Juana, ever wandering with the body
Of her dead husband, frantic in possession,
        Down the harsh roads of Spain
For thirty restless years, in long obsession,
Refusing burial to his mouldered flesh
        While the priests beg in vain.

        All the ripe fruits of life
These mourning women hide in wilful blindness
        Of self-indulgent cloud.
These holy cormorant women, who must swallow
The playful fish of joy; as sharks devour
The happy dolphins, they whose merry movement
Through the translucent water sings aloud.

Kate's stony goodness is reproach to me—
Her life-dismissing misery exudes
The very feel and texture of a shroud.

        How can I live with her? My nature needs
        Abundance of the jollity of life—
        Music and banquet, laughter and applause
        From an admiring and excited crowd.

Grief must have end, however sad the story
        However deep the wound. In its prolonged
Indulgence we become uneasy guests
Sulking in bedrooms in the house of glory.

        Yet have I heard below the silent dawns
        My marriage vows repeating as a bell
        I married her for better or for worse
        The ancient searching dictums won't be shed;
                Repetitive and dull
                They echo like a knell
        So that I cower, foxily, in bed.

        Have done, cold conscience!
        As all men are aware, for Kings the heart
        Must always be the subject of the head.

        Like a black panther lurking in his lair
        The thought is always there—
                She will have no more sons.
        It must be that by nature ***and*** religion
                My marriage is invalid;
        It never was, it never should have been—
        Catharine and I were never truly married.

The Emperor Charles, her nephew, and of Spain
"The King Most Catholic", no fool in state,

Henry

And yet a man who will not hesitate
To loose his forces on the sack of Rome,
Is master of a thunder of great armies
  Strong as a flood in spate
And has but little sympathy for me
Or my desire from his devout good aunt
  Legally to be free.

Though he commands the gold of all Peru
And Mexico, I have now had my fill,
More than my fill of harsh Iberia.
  I look for something new
  And something nearer home
A mate more tuneful to my rousing spirit
And its robust and vital overspill.

* * * *

Reader

For Wyatt the pains of love are growing sharper,
All he can do is sing and play the lute
  To ease his steady ache.
He's gravelled by the madness of ambition
In Anne's wild breast, and sadly seeks to make
The cure that came from mad King Saul's sweet harper
Young David, sent to save him from perdition.
  So Thomas sadly twangs,
Although the notes scarce answer his condition.

Wyatt

"My lute awake! Perform the last
Labour that thou and I shall waste,
  The end that I have now begun:
For when this song is sung and past
  My lute be still, for I have done.

"Perchance thee lie withered and old
The winter nights that are so cold,
Plaining in vain unto the moon:
Thy wishes then dare not be told.
  Care then who list, for I have done.

And then may chance thee to repent
The time that thou hast lost and spent
To cause thy lovers sigh and swoon:
Then shalt thou know beauty but lent
And wish and want as I have done."

* * * *

Reader

Semper eadem—so ran Spain's great motto,
To thine own self be true;
So was Queen Catharine—never to be changed
By any change of mood,
By any wind of heresy that blew.

Henry

Semper eadem—always just the same
Morning and noon and night, early and late,

And that, by God, was all too true of Kate.

Was I alone at fault, growing unkind
Before those set ideas, that changeless mind?

Companionship by rote—
A rigid stiffness brought
From that closed Spanish court
No subtlety, no laughter, and no jokes,
She harped forever on a single note
Holy, but just a mite monotonous.
She would have made a marvellous fine Abbess
In her habitual black, her hoods and cloaks.

Reader

Mourning perpetually for those lost children
Homesick for her lost home
In rich, triumphant Spain,
With little castles on enormous crags;
Stillness of baking noons, the sound of fountains
Falling in gardens framed in colonades
And stony courtyards bright with marigolds;
And every night, and every sunlit morning
Cool chapels where the worship never flags,
A faith that never fades.
Also an iron hardness, which endures
From seven hundred years
Locked in a pitiless warfare with the Moors.

Henry

The question hung suspended, year on year . . .
Though each was diamond hard for their own side
There was no vulgar argument and strife;
Kate was no bitch, but a right royal wife,
And I had too much pride,
Too great a sense of being the Lord's anointed
To rail at her, however disappointed.

She's a good woman. One I could forgive
If she could bear a son prepared to live.

* * * *

Reader

Wyatt is feeling all the bitterness
Of his rejected love.

Wyatt

"They flee from me that sometime did me seek
With naked foot stalking in my chamber.
I have seen them gentle, tame and meek,
That now are wild, and do not remember
That some time they put themselves in danger
To take bread at my hand; and now they range
Busily seeking with a continual change.

Wyatt

Thanks be fortune, it hath been otherwise
Twenty times better; but once, in speciall,
In thin array, after a pleasant guise
When her loose gown from her shoulders did fall
And she caught me in her arms long and small,
Therewith all sweetly did me kiss
And softly said, 'Deare heart, how like you this?'

It was no dream: I lay broad waking.
But all is turn'd, thorough my gentilness,
Into a strange fashion of forsaking;
And I have leave to go of her goodness,
And she also to use newfangleness.
But since that I so kindly am served
I fain would know what she hath deserved.''

* * * *

Henry

I need a doughty son to hold the state,
To keep the glories and the benefits
My wisdom will create;
Virile enough to hold the Lords in check
Subtle enough to keep the love of the commons,
And to communicate
The certainty that his majestic judgement
Will never lead his country into wreck.

What woman could do this?
One child alone is all to stand between
England and chaos; and that one a girl
Narrow and sad; in all, her mother's child,
Without my zest and my vitality,
Though like her mother, worthy enough and good;
But brittle to command this tameless land
Of men who all too easily turn wild.

A ***son*** I needs must have
Be it well understood
Before it is too late:
And clear enough its written
That such a son will not be born of Kate.

Inspite of her devotions and her tears
Four sons have gone from us in fifteen years.

God's teeth! The Devil's in it!
It was the devil taught us to begin it.

Reader

All imperceptibly the male heart hardens—
Or his does— . . . Ah, poor lady, dressed in black,
Moving so slowly through the palaces
Mourning perpetually for those lost children,

Reader

Followed by ladies black and sad as she,
In melancholy march through sunlit gardens,
Sumptuous in riches, and devoured by lack.

Henry

How, where and by whose weapon, does love die?
For die it surely must
Where no affection overpowers the lust.
Others make do with pity—but not I.
Oh, how her righteousness exhausted me!

That sere, wan face, that once was live and pretty,
Ought to persuade the stoniest heart to pity,
But has the opposite effect on mine;
Reproachful looks taking me flat aback
Sending me scudding on another tack.

Reader

He fashions fine excuses.
For the heart's baser uses.

PART THREE

10

Reader

A black-haired witch on a white horse is prancing
Under the oaks, the noble trees of Windsor
        Over the downs of Kent;
Over the palace floors she's lightly dancing
As though earth's joys were given for all of time
        Were given, and not lent,
And youth were here forever, and sweet content . . .

Henry

And I am spent, am spent.

Reader

Her slim young body bending still, and swaying—
Here is the nymph that flies with sure intent
Her long black eyes discreetly sideways glancing,
Her wit, her skill in every fashion playing
        On the King's ready heart
That is in turn set ruling, or obeying,
        Rejoicing, or dismaying,
        Conquered in every part.

Henry

        I was besotted by her;
Deep in the seas of love, and drowning there.
        Fond as an innocent boy,
        And silly with desire
Her beauty blotting out all other care.

All my fierce purpose, all my iron will
Slowly become directed to one end
Which only this one lady can fulfil—
Legal possession, and a son by her.
        My obligations fade
        All other faces blur . . .

Yes, she was clever, had a pretty wit,
Her thoughts original, her singing voice
        Lilting and pure.
For who could hold a man as sharp as I am
        —Over long waiting years—
With nothing but her sexual allure?

        A daring bright bravado
Lightened her talk, her masking, and her dance.
She read the latest treatise, would discuss
        Delightfully, with charm,
Notions that filled my learned Kate with alarm.
Anne sent for books and music out of France.
The Bible late translated into English,
—Which Thomas More called "filthinesse"—she read
And gave it to her ladies without Latin,
She pleasured in ideas of advance.

Henry

She hunted with a zest
Almost as rash as mine;
So full of sport, and such good company,
In dress and manners and accoutrement
Fashionable and fine.

And in this dark-haired girl
Something of Wallis Simpson was foreshadowed—
Foreign and novel and as smart as paint,
And heartily disliked by other women;
The liveliness, the wit, the repartee,
The difference (not in any manner quaint);
She had the sauce to answer No! and No!
The strength to turn the slender back and go.

And the same subtle skill—
A spider's web a long while in the spinning
Gossamer soft to the touch,
But iron in her ruthless power of winning
The cruel game of life.

What hope in all this for the honest wife?

Challenging, teasing, strange, and self-assured,
The sweet sophistication of Anne's style
Early un-shipped me.
French graces and French dress allured the eye—
And that rare smile.
(Catherine was always smiling.)
Anne fascinated first, and in a while
Totally gripped me.

Reader

(Once out of their glass case
Kings are most vulnerable
Of all the lovers in the human race.)

Soon, all too soon, the lady had him cold
Like a great salmon laid upon a slab,
Drowning and gasping, till he could have died—

For five long years thirsting, half-satisfied.

Aut Caesar, then, ***aut nihil***; this was clear.
She would be Queen or would have nothing of him
Year after longing year.

* * * *

Reader

And what of Wyatt, and maybe other lovers
Now dumped within the dustbin of the past,
Kept at arm's length, till Anne is in the clear?
Are they too frightened ever to come near?

Reader

The cunning aphrodisiac of power
        Has lured his love away,
Will Wyatt challenge, or play the stricken deer?

Peril came early. On the bowling green
Where they had just enjoyed a happy exchange
And paced to where their shots would soon be lying
Sharp between Thomas and the King was known
        Rivalry yet unseen
        Over this girl beguiling.
Spying Anne's jewels worn about each other—
"Wyatt, I tell thee that the shot is mine"
Says the King to him, dangerously smiling,
And seeming less the gamesman and the brother.

        No fool, Thomas will know
        The limit of his range,
        And the sureness of her change
Since so explicitly she's told him so.

Yet seeing this sure sign
Of the King's purpose, and his victory,
The devil of sexual jealousy enters in—
Wyatt will not at once his love release
        Cost what it may;
And stubbornly contrived a kind of tease
        In answer to the King,
Measuring distance with his jewelled chain
        That wore Anne's ring
        He said, ***his*** shot would roll
        The nearest to the mark
        And ***his*** the winning bowl.

There was no need of further explanation
Both understood; both curbed their indignation.
Now the King knew the force of Wyatt's claim
        He spurned aside the bowl
"It may be so, but then I am deceived".
        And always laughing, so broke up the game.

* * * *

Reader

        Terrible laughter.
        Wyatt, who had been
As usual, merry-hearted, stood there still,
        On the bare bowling green
In a confusion between rage and shame.

Henry

So Wyatt, in the torment of negation,
Night in his flesh and tumult in his head
When Anne perceived my steady gaze upon her
        And quietly left his bed,
In bitterness sums up the situation
        In the release of verse.

Wyatt

"Whoso list to hunt, I know where is an hind
But as for me, alas, I may no more
The vain travail has wearied me so sore
I am of them that furthest come behind;
Yet may I by no means my wearied mind
Draw from the Deere, but as she fleeth afore
Fainting I follow. I leave off therefore
Since in a net I seek to hold the wind.

Who list her hunt, I put him out of doubt
As well as I, may spend his time in vain:
And graven with Diamonds in letters plain
There is written her fair neck round about
Noli me tangere, for Caesar's I am
And wild for to hold, though I seem tame."

Reader

Wyatt now faces a dire quandry.
Since the King probably intends to marry
His lost love Anne,
He rightly fears that if the King discover
That Wyatt indeed has some while been her lover
His life and goods are likely to miscarry.

Wyatt

Divided thoughts of honour rake me through—
Never to kiss and tell. There's also faith,
Fidelity, and loyalty, to ***Kings***
Above the private honesty of man,
Against my gratitude and love for Anne.

To tell would be to rouse the wrath of Howards
(Hatred of such an ilk is rarely seen.)
And enmity in a potential Queen,
Of all most dangerous things.

Better lie low than risk the rage of Kings.

But lying low is not my favourite habit.

Never to kiss and tell; a gentleman
Imbibes such maxims with his mother's milk.
But there's a King, and there's a higher duty,
Faith not to be suborned
However in my person hurt and scorned,
By craven fear, or the sharp pull of beauty.

Reader

Wyatt alone, mastered a deadly fear.
In prescience mingled with temerity
He told the King the news he would not hear.

Henry

And what a sliding was of courage then
From all those doughty fellows!

Henry

Such fear of vengeance over what had been
At one time, all among the guilty pillows!
For only Wyatt dared to tell the truth
That he, and others, knew too good a reason
Why Anne should not be Queen.

Wyatt

And not by hearsay either, to my shame.

Henry

This I would not believe.
Standing awhile, in thought,
—A silence far more ominous than speech—
Not raging, not apportioning the blame
I told him to be silent, then and ever,
And not again to utter such a claim.

In all this, Wyatt stood courageous friend.
The others, fawning courtiers, feared to wreck
Precarious favour under storms of rage
Dreading my perilous fury to engage.

Reader

But he, maybe, foresaw the bloody end—
The fatal axe falling on that slim neck;
Knowing how boldly Anne would chance her arm
To be where she would be
In sumptuous majesty.

Wyatt

As I would, and discount the future harm.

Henry

Yet still my blinded eyes
Refusing to see anything amiss
In sweet and lively Anne,
Groped forward to this long-desired bliss.
All my ambition centred on one wish
Was turned towards one dark and teasing girl—
Blow hot, blow cold, blow tender, blow aloof,
By day, by night, tormented and oppressed—
She played me as an angler plays a fish.

God, and the world as well, must know the rest
Of my tale, and of Anne's, and of much more—

Reader

"She that did set our country in a roar!"

* * * *

Wyatt

Now safely out of love
We shrewder fellows noted her designs;
And I, still courtier, and still a poet
Summed up the turgid business in two lines—
"To love and not be wise
Is but a mad devise."

Reader

In the first flush of love
Who knows, and who will care
How grimly passion spent exacts her fines.

Now all of Europe will become involved
In what should be these private battle lines.

Wyatt, recovered, went with them to Kent
Henry the King, and Anne, now Lady Pembroke
A new-made Countess, glamorous and strong.
Wyatt himself new-born—

Wyatt

"Lo! how desire is both sprung and spent
And he may see that whilom was so blind,
And all his labours now he laughs to scorn."

Reader

Men suffer in their love;
Suffer indeed. But do not suffer long.

11

Henry

All through our fighting years, the subtle Charles
Had asked for more, co-operated less
In my ambitions to be King of France
As were my forbears;
Till, in my distress,
Crossly I cried, with realism's birth,
"The winning of Thèrouanne has cost me more
Than twenty such ungracious dogholes' worth!"

Seeing too late that the France that I would win
Would be to me no land of milk and honey,
That all the Emperor wanted was my money.

"Obstinate silence" in the Commons, too
Met my demands for cash and still more cash.
Cold in the fields of France
My soldiers shouted "Home!"
Even to me, the plan
Became impossible as well as rash.
But this is not the end.
Let no-one think that as a Conquering King
I've cut my final dash.

Wolsey

Now Wolsey, in this complicated dance
Takes at the Emperor's hand a mighty toss.
Promised the Papacy and getting nothing,
Decides to cut our loss;
Turning from Emperor Charles
And taking by the hand the King of France.

Henry

I was the first to call the whole thing off,
And from this war
Took what there was of fame.
Wolsey, most naturally, acquired the blame.

Since Charles repudiates his long engagement
To wed my daughter—here's the sharp affront
On a grand scale.
So let the Emperor now
Pay his huge debts; the while I marry Mary
To the French Dauphin, and confirm my vow.
It would much more avail
Valois and Hapsburg kings to keep apart,
Though Wolsey take the brunt,
As do those Englishmen who loathe the French,
Transference without pause
While Catharine and her daughter break their heart—
She loves her nephew and his lantern jaws.

As to my marriage, and the needful son,
Wolsey was angling for some great Princess
To balance any continental loss.

Well, let him angle, and take another toss.

I have a different plan
Centred upon the dark-haired wench called Anne.

Wolsey's forgotten how my grandfather
Edward of York, married his wife for love,
While Warwick angled for a great Princess
Called Bona of Savoy.
Where are the riches of the Continent
Measured with sexual joy?

And now the wheel of fortune takes a turn
To Wolsey's sorrow, and my great content.

* * * *

Henry

How honest had my marriage really been?
"My Lord", said Thomas Wyatt to the King
"Cannot a man repent him of his sin
Without the leave of the Pope?"
He spoke in jest, with flippancy. And yet
The words sink in.

It was the French who brought the matter up
Seriously, in fifteen twenty-seven,
The Bishop of Tarbes
Asking if Princess Mary, whom they sought
As bride for the young Dauphin, had been born
In lawful wedlock? Since they knew Queen Catherine
Had first been married to my brother Arthur.
If not, the project was to come to nought.

Reader

Gabriel de Grammont, Bishop of Tarbes in France
Is credited by Henry with the notion
(That probably arose
In his own agile brain,
Where it intently grows
And causes international commotion)—
That his own marriage to Catherine is invalid,
Since she had first been married to his brother.

Henry

Pope Julius had no right, nor any other,
Such marriage to allow;
How false was such a vow!
I never have, in point of fact been married.

Its easier to blame the Frenchman Bishop
For this mischance.
And even to myself, as well as Wolsey,
To lay the indiscretion
At the insouciant door
Of Francis, King of France.

How the French love to denigrate and question!
Hearing of it, the Queen was most forlorn,
And I incensed, not to say furious
To find the French so insolent and curious.
But thinking the whole thing over
First Wolsey, and then I, with differing plans
Lept with avidity on this suggestion.
If my first marriage really was invalid
I'll be in clover.

The Bishop of Lincoln, backed by many priests
Had then declared my marriage ''damnable'';
And here's a matter for the Pope's digestion.

Alas for hopes! In this same year, in May,
A dreadful shock went shuddering all through Europe—
The Emperor Charles, Queen Catherine's long-faced nephew
Allowed the sack of Rome
With all its holiness, with all its treasures—
Rape, robbery, and murder to appal,
A frantic devastation.
This brought the matter home
To Papal heart, Papal advisers all:
Keep in with Charles and with his wronged relation!

Here's the true cause for Christendom to fear—
Beyond the niceties of canon law
That leave my path unclear—
The Holy City savaged
The Papal forces treed,
Down every screaming street

Henry

Spanish and Austrian soldiery compete
To slake their lust and wrath
And gratify their greed.
Sieged in the great Castello
The Pope himself, poor fellow,
In danger of his life.
Rome is more rudely ravaged
Than since the days of Alaric the Goth.

These are the hosts of Charles
The Emperor of the ***Holy Roman Empire***
And Lord of mighty Spain
"Most Catholic of Kings",
Who do these savage things.

And hardly qualified to turn on me
With cries of, Heresy!

Reader

Henceforth his efforts will be all in vain
To further his divorce.
Popes are not lacking in sagacity
Though they be so in military resource:
No Pope will risk displeasing Charles again.

The Germans and the Spaniards, raising hell
Throughout the Holy City, rang the knell
On any hope of swift divorcing measures.

Henry

I'm still convinced my marriage must be cursed.
Whence all those infant deaths? For in my ages
Men were most prone to superstition's rages.

Reader

Not yet acquainted with the ***rhesus factor***
They thought the Devil himself must be the actor.

Henry

I am not to be deterred.
Might not one Pope's decision be reversed
By his successor?
Might not my youthful marriage be annulled
By lots of money and a little pressure?

And here, at last, I found my limitations,
Deadlocked within the Papal hesitations.
Never quite saying either No, or Yes,
Even suggesting that a Pope might bless
A marriage, once accomplished, to my love
Even without divorce (which Popes have granted
Often enough, for good dynastic reasons.)
So why accept this ***firman*** from above?

So passed the weary unproductive seasons . . .
And all the while my heart was held enchanted.

Reader — Divorce is not yet won, not even starting.

Henry —
And now I miss her badly—
"The woman in the world I value most . . . "
I wrote to Anne when she withdrew from Court,
Lamenting sadly
"The loneliness I have since your departing".

Reader —
By what strange moon's attraction does the tide
Of passion rise and fall?
Are ***we*** in charge at all?

Henry —
There was a kind of promise made that autumn
When 'Fabius Cunctator' (or the Pope)
Wiped sympathetic eyes
And sighed, and said how much he wished he could
Do more to help. And lastly sent Campeggio
—An ailing Cardinal—
To try the case in ***England***, as he should.

Reader —
Campeggio, suffering terribly from gout
Arrived, and tried to put dispute to rout.

Why not, perhaps, a dignified retreat
Into a nunnery of queenly grandeur?
The Papal words entreat.
But Catherine will have none, and crosses swords;
She firmly baulks at any compromise,
Calls it hypocrisy, demands her rights,
Sends secret messages to nephew Charles
Begging for help; and rapidly obtains
All that this powerful Emperor affords.

Henry —
Deadlock again.
God's teeth, the deathly fanatics of Spain!
Pedro the Cruel, Henry the Impotent,
And mad Juana, what a royal stock
Whose pride will ***not*** unlock!
Their glories don't suggest
A way of life the noblest and the best.
Even brave Ferdinand, brave Isabella
Made a religious cleansing without measure
Of Moors and Jews long settled in their land,
Whilst keeping all their treasure!

Catherine is stubborn still.
She sings the same old note
Whatever mediators may suggest,
She answers them by rote—
"I was a virgin, and my marriage true".
Against such marble righteousness
What ***is*** the peace-seeking Campeggio,
Or any man, to do?

Henry

Now, slowly, I begin to wish her ill.
Love that was true, turning to enmity
        That all may see,
Though never to the wicked wish to kill.

*   *   *   *

Henry

I want my spiritual money back.
For Rome has somehow tarnished her refulgence
With treacheries and schisms, and her sack
By Emperor Charles.
                Too many men abandon
A power made suspect by its sold indulgence
And ceaseless greed for gain.
The Papacy's grown weak;
        Not enough legs to stand on.

But I, Henricus Rex, am firm and strong;
And if I go on long enough contending
The vacillating purpose may be bending,
Screws may be turned, or keys may yet unlock
        The happy ending.

Reader

        Great good may yet ensue:
There's nothing like the therapy of shock
To turn St Peter back into the rock
From which the stream of holiness comes wending
Wider and free-er, more humane and true.

Humane! through many years of tragedy
While Europe undergoes a lengthy torment—
Two-sided persecution, an obscene
Dragon of fire and rack and hideous gutting
        Walking the well-loved land—
The burning Protestants on Smithfield Green,
Cold councillors on mass destruction bent,
The rigid anger of the Council of Trent,
Clamour and treachery and cruel intent;

The massacre of Saint Bartholomew,
Brave tortured Jesuits, and ever new
Fierce anguish of the Thirty Years of War,
Avenging armies that will not be stayed
Or turned from their self-righteous cavalcade;
Religious cleansing of Bohemia
Till none but Catholics may there abide,
        Cromwell in Ireland on the other side;
War without mercy between Christian men
        War without pity and without respite
The streaming grace of Jesus Christ our Saviour
Transmogrified into the Devil's tide,
The brilliant day of learning turned to night,

Reader
Through long, long years . . .
Until the passion to condemn is fled
And tolerance can lift her gentle head.

Henry
Some conflicts have to come.

Reader
Too many men resented Papal rule.

Unlikely persons are the catalyst
Raising the devils whom they cannot school
Nor order to desist.
Crafty ambitious dames,
The angry or the idealistic man,
Through rising passions, or by armoured fist
Launch the affray—
Henry the King, the student Gavril Princip,
Dowager Empress ruling in Cathay,
The bearded Lenin hidden in his train,
Mahatma Gandhi, and the long-necked Anne;
In part, the faithful and the stubborn Kate
The haute Princess of Spain;
Powerless and powerful and unlikely beings
Such various shapes of clay
Let loose the dogs of war,
Unknowingly precipitate the pain.

* * * *

Henry
Why should Pope Clement lead me such a dance?
No-one can say I haven't served Rome well—
Writing my learned treatise against Luther,
Defending Julius from the infidel
When "the most Christian King" was with the Turk.
Of my divorce, why such a piece of work?

When not long since, two of the Kings of France
Were by the Pope allowed it; when my sister
The flighty misbehaving Margaret
The widowed Queen of Scotland, wed to Angus
And tiring of him, was allowed divorce—
These matters treated as a thing of course.

Why won't he now decide it
For me, Defender of the Christian Faith?
Delay . . . Delay . . . Delay . . . And still delay.
What Prince of Christendom would long abide it?

And all this while, for Anne
I die of love, suffocate in frustration.
For she will be
No mistress, to be subject to rejection,

Henry — Only a wife, and queen of all my realm
As well as my affection.

Past-mistress of the tease,
Her all-but of submission
Has fettered me forever on my knees.
And this is a position
To which I'm little used.

How came I, to be meekly thus abused?
Given so little rope?

Reader — Commons and Kings have quarrelled with the Pope
Often enough—but this time is unique.
This time the English king is far from weak.

Reader — Alas for Henry!
There is a time, before the draught is taken
When the true self sees clear; is not forsaken.
Swallowing that first drop
Of warm attraction, ready sympathy,
We cancel our capacity to stop.

Adultery committed in the heart
Lays its unresting siege; and it is here
Within the mind's exuberant excess
That uncontrollable seductions start.

The tyranny of the accomplished deed,
The evil done forever, bears its seed;
Scatters and spreads, blown over his rich ground,
Flourishes in him like a rampant weed.

Henry — I'm no old woman to believe in witches,
But there's no doubting
Some devil entered into me with Anne,
And lives there, silently but fiercely shouting;
That when those long dark eyes with drooping lashes,
The silver laughter, and the sweet mouth pouting
Made me her haunted slave,
Something within me hardened there forever;
Suffering change
From the youth who loved, and trembled, and had tears,
The youth whom men forgave.

And the boy's heart, that once was Kate's alone
Within my lusty body turned to stone.
All that was fallible, persuadable,
That once would argue with such "gentilness",
And yield with such an "affability
Of temper", such a "sweetness of address",
Deserted me, to harden on my own.

12

Henry

Fabius Cunctator still prevails in Rome,
Clement the Seventh and the Undecided.

No answer comes to my divorce petition
My envoys thwarted by a blank audition—
God's death! who do they think I am?

Never say die, and never say surrender.
(And never, young men, let yourself be tied
At eighteen years, to marry with one woman.)

Using the love I easily engender
Among my countrymen, I'll show the world
Exactly who in Britain holds the helm.

Reader

Campeggio has summoned a great court
With strict instructions not to reach conclusion.
But Henry is resolved to get in first—
Recipe for confusion;
Surely, the thing's accurst?

Henry

I summoned all the great men of the realm
In fifteen twenty-eight, in chill November,
To meet with me at Bridewell in the City.
Nobles, the Mayor, the aldermen, the merchants,
Summoned to Bridewell, stood with bated breath,
Waiting a great assault upon their pockets.
This is no money matter—
For this is life and death.

I've reigned, I said, for twenty years with honour,
With wealth and victory, "but I must die . . .
When we remember our mortality"
(And here I conjured up a heavy sigh)
"The doings of our lifetime are defaced . . .
If our true heir be not knowen at our death . . .
Then shall succeed to you and all your children . . .
The mischiefs and the manslaughters of old . . . "

And this went home to all these anxious men
Whose straining eyes were concentrated on me.
Collective blood ran cold
Thinking of those dynastic wars again.

Thus far, I spoke from the heart, with true intent,
Thereafter, bluff and humbug thickly blent.

"I would be thankful", I informed them all
"If clergy would pronounce the Queen my wife"
In full legality of Church and State;
Speaking the words with full majestic weight.

Henry

Then dwelt a pause, to see how these words went.
(So easily we fool ourselves at will
That at that moment I believed the whole
And trembled at the danger to my soul
In daring to co-habit with Queen Kate.)

Far back, I heard a choked and nervous titter,
Stopped by a long and devastating pause.

My steady gaze embraced them, dared their answer,
And held them silent with its dangerous glitter.
Within my mind a wary calculation,
Ready and cool, poised lightly as a dancer,
Quick to defend my cause.

(To sway the minds of men, confuse, and fool them,
To bend them, all unconscious, to sheer will,
Offers the heart enormous satisfaction,
And settles many scores.)

This was as dear a wife as man could find,
I told them, and a very great Princess,
"And of great gentilness and buxumness".
I stopped for emphasis, then let them have
The matter whole—

"Great clerks have told me that I live in sin . . .
Think you, my lords, that these their words touch not
My body and my soul? . . .
These be the sores that deeply vex our mind.
And for these griefs I seek a remedy."

Spellbound, they drank it in.
And stood impressed;
And went away believing
(Or so in my great hardihood I guessed.)

None of them had forgotten
Wars of the Roses, and their long unease
The times of fearful "mischiefs and manslaughter".
And just such wars might trouble all this realm
Perhaps to dispossess my tender daughter
Whom some named misbegotten.

Reader

Christmas, the season of disport and holly
Was passed at Greenwich; but the unhappy Queen
Finally banished from the marriage bed
Laid on a truly massive Spanish scene
And the whole time was tinged with melancholy.

But as a kind of weapon in the fight
Campeggio's bastard son I dubbed a knight.

* * * *

Henry

Better to re-assure the worthy Commons
Inclined in favour of fidelity
And somewhat shocked at my neglect of Kate—
"I'm forty-one", I told the wary Speaker,
"At which age
The lust of man is never yet so quick
As in his lusty youth".
But this urbane reply
Though an acknowledged truth,
The Papal disapproval won't assuage.

Absolute need, I felt, to change the weather
To something sunlit, irresponsible.
Playing Anne's brother, I was beat at dice
And lost a lot of money. Long past reason,
Past caution or discretion or advice,
I sent my love a nightdress of black satin.

"Return to Catharine" Clement sternly wrote,
"Embrace your Queen, or excommunication
Will fall on you". I read the sombre Latin
Implacably; for I had been to France.
Allied with Francis, I was not afraid.

Here was a risk I could afford to take.

"Fisherman, fisherman", I told the Pope,
"Pull your nets softly, they are like to break".

* * * *

Reader

The legates come and go, argue, debate,
And nothing really happens all the while.
The matter came to set and solemn trial
Next June, before a bishop-ridden court,
Two Cardinals preside in chairs of state—
Campeggio and Wolsey.

And in this same month
Queen Catherine had been to see Campeggio
(Who lay in bed with gout)
And sworn she'd bedded only seven times
With young Prince Arthur, and to no effect.
So what was this absurd divorce about?

Henry

The morning dawned for this affair of state.
I strode before them with my confident gait,
Mind ready to confront and overwhelm.

Rightly did handsome Suffolk bellow out

Suffolk

That "it was never merry in this realm
Since Cardinals came in".
Eyes turned on them—and mostly upon Wolsey—

Suffolk These proud red-hatted princes of the Church
Risen from lowly birth and dazed by splendour,
One beedy eye fixed on the Papacy
The other on the purse,
Men worldly and untender.

Reader Is the worst sin
That icy and unsleeping lust for power
By which the Devil fell from his high state?
Denied the outlet of man's natural joy
More dangerous lust attacks the celibate
Than comes from marriage day,
Or even any tumble in the hay—
A ruling passion to manipulate.

Henry They sat, red-robed, and ringed, and authorized,
And if I felt disquiet, it was unseen.

Called out to witness, I responded calmly
"No man" I told the court "had better Queen".
My long stare challenged men to look surprised.
"But this is pain, unquietness" in belief
"That I discover that I live in sin
With a brother's wife. My conscience seeks relief.
I cannot govern with a mind so troubled"
Throughout my mortal span.

Then Catherine rose, and slowly knelt before me,
And a great sigh, like wind in standing corn,
Troubled the court; and died as she began;
And everyone was still.

Here was direct appeal
The look that can't dissemble—
The troubled searching language of the eyes
From the old love to the forsaking lover;
As if somewhere, deep as the years can hide it
Or carelessness conceal,
She might discover
The ghost of those old happy days together,
And even resurrect
A heart that still could tremble to be near her,
Spirit that yet might feel.

Reader Vain hope! that she'll correct
And turn him back to her with such a look—
For the forsaking lover can't abide it.

Catherine "Sir I beseech you"
Reader The deep voice began,
Still breathy with the consonants of Spain,

Catherine

"For all the love that there hath been between us
Let me have justice, let me have my right,
And take of me some pity and compassion
For I am a poor woman, and alone",
        Friendless and far
        From an unbiased judge,
"A stranger, born away from your dominions . . . "

Reader

A plea that might have moved a heart of stone.

Henry

Yet stonily I still deny her right,
Hardily gaze un-moving at the plight
That throws this Queen thus suppliant before me;
        For, to be candid.
        Such histrionics bore me.

For how can Kate go nursing my dead love?
        As her sad sister
Poor mad Juana, nurses her long dead lord
Forever down the dusty roads of Spain
        The battered coffin swinging heavily
        Nor ever finding rest,
        Though all about her faint.
Whence this determined and un-seeing love
        This single-hearted zest
        Of these two loyal sisters?
        This self-inflicted pain
        From devil or from saint?

Love of my sort is not for resurrection.
Serious intelligence, a mind well-stocked,
A kindly nature, and embroidered shirts,
        Have never been enough
To harness the imponderable heart
Of an attractive and much younger man,
        Too wildly rocked
By beauty and excitement, to discover
The callous ***rigor mortis*** of its stuff.

Reader

And so the piteous kneeling Queen went on—

Catherine

"As God is witness, I am your true wife"
And humble, and obedient to your will.
"When first you had me—God will be my judge—
I was a true maid, without touch of man . . . "

Henry

The eyes of all observers looked upon me
Who only could give answer to the Queen—
        And gave her none.

        My eyes, expressionless
        Told no more than my tongue;

Henry	Would not deny, or bless, Spoke only pride, Dislike of all this intimate exposure; As if that gallant, that once loving Henry Lusty, rejoicing, young, Had long since died.
Catherine	The ghost of those dead children loomed unseen, All the remembered tears, our joint despair, Hung in the stifling air.
Henry	But I could only see the face of Anne And I could only feel The movement of her body under mine, And my heart froze against the supplication Of that poor lady under Fortune's heel; That cry from days when we were Kate and Harry, Before her poor heart broke.
Reader	Those melancholy eyes continued pleading, Her sad voice spoke—
Catherine	"I put it to your conscience what has been When we did marry."
Henry	Still my impervious lips betrayed no sign. Behind flat eyes my mind rehearsed its grudge. Catherine had done. With a deep reference to me, she was gone.
Catherine	In proud contempt of courts that dare pronounce On royalty, whom God alone may judge, I swept away from all, Among the murmurs, and the women's chatter. "On, on!" I cried to them, "it makes no matter Tis an indifferent court to me, I will not tarry".
Henry	And so she left the Hall— Black-garmented, and alien, and unlovely, Too plump and much too small— Never more noble, never more a Queen; Certain that we were man and wife forever And no man's court had power to intervene, Nor her troth sever.
Reader	And a brief silence fell upon us all.
Henry	And in our hearts that distant roll of thunder "Whom God hath joined, let no man put asunder".
Reader	Churchmen, ambassadors, had pleaded with her, The very Popes in their replies had altered;

Reader

All powers of statecraft had been launched against her,
Lies, and excuses, and the law's way round,
Measures above board, methods underground,
She only, never would gainsay her creed,
        She only, never faltered;
She only on this day was Queen indeed.

        And Suffolk's raucous laughter
At Cardinals, and all the echoing voices,
        Were subtly altered.

* * * *

Henry

Did I love Catherine? Yes I loved her once;
        Coming in splendour out of Aragon
And wedded to my brother; she was fair
Dowered and beautiful in early hope—
Grey eyes, fidelity, the queenly air,
The pride, some of the cruelty of Spain . . .

Poor grievous faithful Queen, how hard she tried!
My youth rebelled against her useless pain
        The heart began to harden in my breast.
Three stillborn sons, another one who died—
        The grief of it, again, and yet again.

Reader

And why? Even an age less superstitious
Would have surmised that something must be wrong.

Henry

Yes, I was hot, and weary, and impatient,
And clouded with success and adulation
My driving purpose was a healthy son . . .
Why did the matter linger on so long
In Rome, where other Princes gain divorces
        For sound dynastic reasons?

        And Anne, sweet Anne Boleyn!
Laughing and dancing through the dreary seasons.
The time stretched endless, my desire was strong.
        Who would not set the cart before the horses
        Tortured by love's long pain?

Henry

        She was my evil genius—long-necked Anne
        With those round breasts, and those oblique black eyes
        Whose dark and bird-winged eyebrows seemed to soar,
        And that determined virtue—which was hollow.
        With every turn of the neck I loved her more.

Reader

And every turn of the tide in distant Europe
Will sweep these lovers further from the shore.

* * * *

Henry

The argument meanders to and fro.
Catherine appeals to Rome;
Where I am quite determined not to go.
For there the cauldron bubbles
With eager cardinals alert for bribes,
And wholly unconcerned with England's troubles.

Of Western Christendom
The Pope is still the head.
I'll send my envoys out to Rome instead.

Oh Deuteronomy, Leviticus!
(We all consulted the Old Testament,
Avoiding "public honesty", and sense.)
I was too set on strict legality,
Advanced too many different arguments,
For my divorce to be.
I sent too many men. I tried too hard.
At Rome they whisked away the documents
We needed, and by Catherine's careful agents
My strongest hopes were marred.

And many of the documents we found
For my petition offered little ground.

Frustrated, I would go behind the back
Of Wolsey, my best hope,
By sending writs that never met his eyes:
Or try another tack.
In short by giving lawyers too much rope
Hanged the whole enterprise.

Be very sure of this—
Even if Anne Boleyn had not been born
Even if Rome had granted my divorce
I would have had my way
And set the Church upon another course.
The echoes ringing yet through Bury Abbey
Where the knights met to sign the Magna Carta
In long since twelve fifteen,
Came sounding home to me—
"Libera sit, Ecclesia Anglicana",
Ecclesia Anglicana, be it free!

This suited both my temper and my purpose.
Over the years, these hardened,
And the break came to be.

I sought return to the first early Christians
With their autonomous churches
And their simplicity.

Henry

And with Erasmus and Sir Thomas More
The flagrant riches of the priests deplore,
Their gold, their jewels, their abundant land.
How could the poorer followers of Christ,
        Christ homeless, and un-moneyed,
Such Midas concentration understand?

        Tradition. Reason.
        We need something new,
We need the reading of the Gospels too,
This many people had begun to mutter.
        We need to clear the clutter
Of a church that for too long has shut the door
On daylight, and too firmly slammed the shutter.

13

Henry

Wolsey was useful once; I needed him
To do the donkey work and make things better.
Clever, industrious Wolsey, taking blame
For wars where my ambition was the frame,
Ruinous wars with France.

        Now he is grown too great;
Lives like an Emperor, owning half the State
And ruling hundreds with his mighty name.

Having accepted half the great possessions
        He had acquired by stealth,
Sent humbly, to propitiate my wrath,
I sent him presents, let him rule in York
        Still owning princely wealth.

Little it gives me ease
That France, Spain, Netherlands are now at peace;
        For still untaught
The Pope revokes the judgment of my Court
        Divorcing me from Catherine,
        And calls Campeggio home.

        I sped him from my shores
With private rudeness, and with outwardly
        A silver tongue,
        In observations short;
With this pronouncement for the Pope's confusion—
        "My subjects are ill-pleased
That this my case has found no good conclusion".

        Though Anne most sharply hated clever Wolsey,
        While coveting his wealth, I still did not.

Reader

"There's great decay, ruine and povertie",
And, people cry, Wolsey has done the harm!
"Advancing his own high and prodigal palm",

And now a nobleman conspiracy
Would jostle this fine minister from power;
Wolsey disdained,
As base-born arrogant priest.
Norfolk complains of his faint-heartedness
Over the King's divorce: Suffolk at least
Could have kept silence over one who'd helped him
So greatly in his hour of fearful need,
Could think of nothing but the Cardinal's greed
And his array of sumptuous palaces;
Why should he own so much?
Suffolk advanced his reasons
Adding his callous quota, to prevail
Over the ailing man, the wounded heart.

And Rochford, too, was execrating Wolsey
As butcher's son, as base.
But most of these, brave and resplendent lords,
Though with a flying start,
Ran quite as briskly in the rodent race.

Henry, who sent him money
And messages of cheer
Was less pursuant of the Cardinal's downfall
That now loomed near.
And, more confusingly, blew hot and cold
Across his final year.

Henry

I owed him very much, on many grounds.
That wintertide, in fifteen twenty-nine,
Wolsey fell ill. "Now God forbid" I cried
"That he should die!" I sent my doctor to him—
"I would not lose him for twenty-thousand pounds!"

Reader

Alas, the Cardinal! For once recovered
His passion for intrigue defeated reason.
Why can ambition never give up hope?
He treats in secrecy with France and Spain
And was caught writing letters to the Pope
Now advocating halt to my divorce.

Henry

We intercepted all of them, of course
And sent for him to London.
Now, thank God,
Before the treason trial
(In tune with Anne's demands,
A woman unforgiving)
Can sound poor Wolsey's knell,

Henry
Without his blood resting upon my head
The mighty Cardinal is safely dead.
    Alls well that endeth well.

Reader
Ill with the flux, and with extreme despair
He went to lay his bones at Leicester Abbey,
And there to die.
And dying, wished that he had served his God
Diligently as he had served his King;
For God would not have left him in old age.

Wolsey
"Put not your trust in Princes", he would sigh
    "There is no help in them".

Henry
But rallying before he came to die
He named me as

Wolsey
"A prince of royal courage
And princely heart"; a King whose will and pleasure
    He'd lose a fortune rather than deny.
    Indeed, "a royal stem".

Henry
Which voice was speaking truth? the first, the last?
The smooth old utterance of the sycophant
    Mouthing the usual cant?
Or in the truth of near and certain death
    Affection at the last?
I shall believe that generous final breath
And take it for forgiveness of the past.

Reader
    Victim he died of all that princely living
    And nervousness, and sorrow;
    But the great world of state is unforgiving.

* * * *

Henry
Come joy, come grief, come joust or masquerade
    The laws must still be made.
Laws to restrain young men from early marriage
"Till they be potent . . . tall and puissant persons"
To be restrained from marrying old widows;
    Laws about river weirs.
My spiritual hopes endure miscarriage,
    But my government
Has to go on, and has to be conducted
With proper care of all the population
—This great, fat-headed, and impulsive nation—
However my private life is misconstructed.

The law is vital to me, must be with me,
    Changing as I shall change.
If the Pope baulks me, I shall find adherence
    In Christendom's wide range.
Sure as I am, I must be underwritten
By priestly countenance for my divorce.

Henry

So why not ask the Universities
With all their learning, and their mental force?

An unknown Cambridge scholar, Thomas Cranmer,
Suggested, when I met with him in Essex
That in man's high intelligence lies truth—
Let a man look within and follow conscience,
Though fully taught in youth.

A hard and doughty rider from the Shires
This learned man of God was late-ordained.
He'd been too fiercely disciplined in youth
And something in his spirit deeply pained;
A cruel schoolmaster of Nottingham
Had so "appalled and daunted" him in childhood
That this had dowsed his fires.
He suffered often from confused desires,
Though conscience was his "must".
But these uncertainties
Argued to me an openness to trust.

* * * *

Reader

In fifteen twenty-nine, bereft of Wolsey
Henry the King himself begins to rule,
To read anew, and think, and turn the page
To matters scarcely touched by him before,
Beginning a new age
In sacking Wolsey, calling Parliament,
Making Lord Chancellor
That radical, that most Erasmian layman
His friend Sir Thomas More,
That charming and companionable sage.

But More, who knew him well,
Unwillingly accepted such a post
Made the King promise freedom to his conscience,
Never to compel
This vital element to go astray.
A solemn promise
King Henry would betray.

The King had studied Lutheran literature
(Queen Anne most often urging him thereto),
Read Tyndale in translation of the Bible
And shown an appetite for what was new.

One night, at dinner, he informed Chapuys
That Luther had brought many truths to light,
And had he halted at the Sacraments
Would have been largely right.
In war against the Church's great abuses
All hands were needed,
The Emperor should be urged to join the fight!

Reader

The hair of Chapuys must have stood on end
At notion that his master
The Holy Roman Emperor
Should so entirely bend,
Sharing in what Chapuys saw as disaster.

Henry

In autumn twenty-nine I'd called the Commons
(Whom Wolsey had done happily without)
Since I was shrewd enough to enlist the people
My ever chauvinistic islanders
In a resounding anti-foreign shout,
To show them all, as surely as I might
What interfering foreigners are about.

Not that my people
Needed much teaching, ready to obey
In thwarting priests and Frenchmen any day.

Reader

Like that old Earl of Shrewsbury, who when
Accosted by the French Ambassador
For being "ignoble" in not knowing his tongue,
Turned on him as a 'whoreson dogge", and then
Declared that with a word of "pestilent French"
Within him, he would cut it out with a dagger
At peril of his life.
Most Englishmen applauded this old sinner;
But the French Envoy then refused his dinner,
Trembled, and lost his colour, and his swagger,
And was reported "drinking wondrous oft".

Henry

Thus backed by popular feeling
I sent the priesthood reeling,
By stopping them from sending gold to Rome
And giving English bishoprics away
To the Pope's nominees,
What has the Papacy achieved for me?
We need the gold and goodies nearer home.

Slowly but surely, always through the Council
Who, with some help I could manipulate
Aided in time by clever Thomas Cromwell,
I took the reins of state.

Cranmer was not alone in backing me:
Not only Oxford, Cambridge, and the French
(Somewhat encouraged) plumped for my divorce,
Voting maybe, for every kind of reason
According to their lights.

But those old ornaments of Christendom
The ancient colleges of Italy
Ferrara and Bologna, Padua,
To whom I sent,

Henry

Also concurred, as did my Parliament.
(Naturally Spain and Naples under Charles
Were steadfast for Queen Catherine and her rights.)

Some near to hand, and near to heart, defied me.
"Clergy are scarcely subjects in this land"
I thundered out, in fifteen thirty-two,
"Oath to the Pope undoes their oath to me"
I told the Commons, clear for all to see,
        For all to understand,
This should not be!

Reader

In Convocation only a score of men
        —Prepared to risk their life—
        Would not accept
This long disputed marriage as invalid,
        And Catherine no true wife.

Perhaps a score of the rest of them believed
In very truth that the King had not been married.
        And all the rest, relieved,
        Concurred in the general vote,
        For fear of being harried.

Henry

The Church submitted, and I won control;
And Thomas More, my good friend, Thomas More
Lord Chancellor, resigned the Chancellorship,
Having a great attention to his soul.

Some men reviled me, specially the Carthusians;
But kind Queen Catherine, still ***fidelis semper***,
Yet loved me, and still blamed the whole on Anne,
Whom she named concubine, holding that she
Had warped the native goodness of my heart
"Put him in such perverse and wicked temper".

Was the Queen right? Buried sea-deep within
Under my cruelty, my love of fun,
        And my infatuation,
Lived on a conscience—and a sense of sin,
        Drowned by determination
So to continue as I had begun.

Reader

He was no fool; but ridden by self-will.
And in the deeps of the soul
Those reaches that our reason never plumbs
Was there a molten lava of live guilt
Churning and burning till the moment comes
And a great jet of cruelty is spilt?

        Did he so burn?
Or was it but a callous unconcern
That caused those many disregarded deaths?

* * * *

Reader

Affronted now, the Bishop of Rochester
John Fisher, tells the Emperor he should
Leave other things aside
To stem this terrible tide,
And launch invasion of this rebel island,
So to overwhelm
The wilful Henry, and see his aunt restored
To rightful place as Queen.
Yes, even with the sword—
Un-bishoplike, he urged

Fisher

"Your making war now on this King and Kingdom
Or Christ will lose the realm!"

Reader

Fortunately for England
The busy Emperor can't
Just now restore his aunt
By force of arms, since too much other work
Is still involved for him
In fending off the Turk.

Henry

And luckless Fisher must
For such undoubted treason, bite the dust,
For all the goodness of his previous life.
Into some listening ear, and some keen brain
The knowledge of this treachery was dropped.

Fisher, of course, was chopped.

Reader

Mounting the scaffold on a fine June morning
Fisher was dazzled, as the sunshine brightened
So that he scarce could see, and he proclaimed
"Come into the presence of God, and be enlightened,
There your face shall not be confounded",
Quoting it calmly from psalm thirty-four.
Then spoke no more.

Under the glory of bright summer sun
On Tower Hill, the sombre order sounded,
The cruel deed was done,
His head was grounded;
While the birds sang as sweetly as before.

Few people loved the Pope as men love Christ
With the full warmth that glows in the heart of man.
The primacy of Rome was more a habit
Than it was passion; but Rome's jurisdiction
Had all the power of a long-accepted plan,
Less of a lively love.
With what cool courage then would More and Fisher
Accept the sharp curtailment of their span.

Christ in his kindest glory
The God within, around us, and above,

Reader

Answered, we may be sure, with joy and pity
To this peculiar and fixated love.

So also, to the many Protestants,
In the long agony of their burning alive
    —Those steaming shambles—
Felt the clear certainty of hope survive.
(Under Queen Mary, Cardinal Pole, returning,
Described these humble, faithful folk as "brambles",
As so much garden rubbish to be cleared.)
    These too, Christ surely neared
    As their time came—
Moving in love towards them through the flame.

    Love can be wrong,
Exceedingly macabre and perverse.
    But all the same
    True love is never wasted.
These heroes bearing their unbearable pain,
That, with a word of change, they could have halted,
Bequeathed us faith, and liberty of worship,
    The sanctity of truth;
    Freedom to speak and write
    —That unalloyed delight—
One of the fairest joys that men have tasted.
    These in their death
And their fidelity, mankind exalted.

14

Reader

    The fun goes on, at least.
The summer sunlight mellowed over Windsor;
No pause in the festivity and feast
And plaintive music in the hollow halls.

Henry

One night in June, played between private walls,
I saw a skit on the Apocalypse,
And laughed my head off in the well-known bellow
At satire of myself beheading priests.

Black humour, and the cruel pantomime
Both have been with us since the dawn of time.

Each evening saw new mummeries, new pleasures.
Good company, carousels were my passion.
And Anne had introduced a startling fashion
For heavy make-up and fantastic dress,
Gracefully peacocking in stately measures—
I loved her none the less.

Increasingly, I can't be contradicted,
Nor will I be of fallacy convicted.

*   *   *   *

Reader
The axe now fell on one of the realm's best treasures.

More
"Be merry now, with God" Sir Thomas More
Wrote to his daughter Margaret, from the Tower.
"I will not meddle with the world again . . . "

Henry
He would not yield me my supremacy.

More
"No temporal lord should lead the spiritual",
He argued clear and plain,

Henry
The more's the pity.
Even by me Sir Thomas won't be taught:

More
"God keep me in my just opinion
Even to death" he prayed.

Henry
I offered More my pardon, time for thought;
He would not be gainsaid,
Still less would he be bought.

Then to so old a friend
I offered a clean end.

Reader
He died light-heartedly, as one who feared
Nothing but that his faith should be betrayed.
Mounting the scaffold, he could jest aloud
With guards; and with the executioner
Dreadful with mask and axe
He joked about his beard.

More
"I die" he said "as the King's faithful servant,
But God's first".

Reader
And a sigh of pity sprayed
Over the mournful crowd
When on July the sixth the keen axe fell.

Henry
Whatever moved in me I sought to quell.

And yet, within my haughty being's core
My vengeful heart was sore;
Somewhere, the bubble of my triumph burst
To think that I should laugh with him no more.

Still my cool reason must believe him wrong.
An English Council and an English King
Should be, in English matters, sole decider.
The Pope, not I, had wrought this bitter parting
So needless, and so long;
In lives of many and many an honest man,
The cruel hate and horrible bloodshed starting.

* * * *

Reader

Long long ago, "One Shepherd and One Flock"
By our divisions had been made a mock.

Schism had brought about the Faith's eclipse;
Christians divided, like a fleet of ships
Scattered before the gale of man's self-will,
Lost, as such ships must be, with many captains
        Insisting on command;
Papal intransigeance the usual rock
On which a loss of union could be reckoned,
With bearded fellows of Byzantium
        Coming an easy second.

Henry

Schism! You think that ***I*** invented it?
Emperor Charles has sacked the Holy City,
And long ago Byzantium was sacked
At Christian hands; by many an earlier quarrel
The unity of Christendom was split.

Henry sole author of the schism? No!
You cannot take a stubborn people with you
Unless the bulk of them prefer to go.

Reader

And so the storm of cruelty increased
Beating upon the wicked, and the just.

If any man demurred, he might remember
The burning Lollards writhing in the flame
        At Rome's insistent claim.

Henry

        Must I repeat
If any man deny Supremacy
Of Monarch over Church—then die he must.

Reader

        And die a dozen did;
        Most of them good as gold;
A sight to halt the angels on the wing,
        To make the saints despair,
And the sweet birds of summer cease to sing—
The golden boy become the brutal King.

*   *   *   *

Now ably seconded by Thomas Cromwell
I gathered to myself the reins of the Kingdom
Becoming thus supreme in Church ***and*** State.

Reader

Absolute power can totally corrupt.

Henry

I was inclined to be corrupt already;
        No better and no worse
Than brother Powers over the Continent
Who would the vilest sophistries rehearse.

Henry

I'm adept at hypocrisy and guile,
Breaking a promise with the blandest smile,
    But so will all of them
    Cardinals, Popes and Kings.
I'm honest when its possible; when cornered
I follow the Italian Machiavel,
    And do it just as well.

Tyrant, you say, and cruel. But understand
I lived within the ethic of my day.
Nor ever killed a soul with my own hand.

Look, for a while, at my contemporaries—
Ivan the Dread in Muscovy, Shah Abbas
In Persia, or consider Mogul horrors
In India; of the Turks, Selim the Grim,
    I don't compare with him!
Nor with King Philip in the Netherlands
    Killing whole populations
    Border to border.

True, I condemned a score of men to the axe
    In proper order
    After a trial (of sorts),
But Suleyman, called the Magnificent,
    In fifteen twenty-six
After the dreadful battle of Mohacs
Put fifteen hundred prisoners to the sword;
    Where shore and river mix—
The Danube crimsoned with Hungarian blood.
I poisoned nobody; nor did I order
A holocaust, a Saint Bartholomew,
Killing the followers of Christ's religion
As, soon, would the "Most Christian King" of France.

I had a quarrel; but did not begin it
As did the Popes, refusing
A normal and legitimate request.
And in intrigue, these all could give me best.
I bent the Law sometimes, but lived within it.

*   *   *   *

Henry

"The Kings of England never have been subject
To any jurisdiction upon earth",
Since I was twenty I've been thundering out.
Plantagenet was right and Becket wrong;
And most of us have known this all along.
The Pope who first un-wrote the Magna Carta
Was wrong, and came in time to rue the day.

    And I am master here
By right of potency, by right of birth—
    Master I'll stay.

Henry

And furthermore, to make the verdict clear—
If the Pope will not stir in my divorce,
　　　　I've weapons of my own—
Diplomacy, and money, and my wits,
My cunning, fraud, and force.

The Prelate holding Christendom in fee
Persuading me to marry Anne Boleyn
Without divorcing Catherine, surely errs?
Winking at mortal sin? And it was then
　　　　He lost, for me
His vital spiritual authority.

　　　　And as to Mother Church
This cannot be the Mother that men seek!
Priests, being human beings, have to stumble,
Although the Holy Spirit cannot falter,
And laymen, being people, have to grumble,
But our disquiets are more than day-to-day—
Monks sunk in laziness and nuns astray
Must be, perhaps; but what we find unique—
Great worldly churchmen of enormous wealth
Giving their benefices to their bastards,
Playing at international bezique,
And bargaining alliance all the way
　　　　For ultimate preferment;
Games better fit for statesmen and for kings
Who must accept the practise of such things,
Move swiftly, or take refuge in deferment.

All this is odious in a Church conceived
To help the humble and exalt the meek,
To banish pride, and turn the other cheek.

Reader

This sad and furious disquietude
Is echoed in a continental mood.
Something, it is accepted, has gone wrong;
But must the Church go on in stubborn error
　　　　For quite so long?

Henry

An arrogance of purpose now possessed me
But all the while, some vein of common sense
Ran deep within, bidding me to be still,
　　　　Telling me when to halt,
And thus to keep the love of common people;
　　　　Some canny Welshman prescience
　　　　Held me from fatal fault.

"Never more wilful than in carnal love"
Wrote Cavendish, of the strong will of princes.
And now I take the Kingdom in my hands,
　　　　Loosed of all Papal bands.

Henry

Yet still I speak and act as from the Council
As with the will of priests and lawyers, lords,
And aldermen and mayors, all agreeing
        To this conspicuous freeing,
        Thus I use
All the strong backing that the state affords.

How did I do it—judge, you faithful Commons,
How this enormous change was made in peace
        Without a standing army, or police.

* * * *

Reader

Pole had sent Henry a long admonition
        That could not have been ruder,
Calling the King, "a Nero, a Domitian,
More enemy to Christ than were the Turks".
His mother, much revered, sent Pole reproof;

Lord Montague

"No prudence and no pity" blamed his brother,
(Lord Montague, affrighted and aloof),
"An running from one mischief to another".

Bishop Tunstall

Even mild Tunstall wrote "your bloody book
Pricketh me, makes me heavy in the heart".
        Henry's reply was mild;
He hoped that Pole might thus return to England
        By gentleness beguiled.
But the incipient cardinal was shrewder.

* * * *

Long love implies long knowledge, and the Queen
        Pled with me still by letter
        With her unwearied zest—
Catharine, perhaps indeed she knew me better
        Than I myself?
        Perhaps she knew me best.
I might have answered to that deep affection
        And treated her more kindly
Even have spared the noblest monasteries,
Had she not used our marriage as a fetter.

* * * *

Reader

And so this long intractable impasse
Over my marriage, still unmoving stood
Through all these years. The snows of six long winters
Hardened along the hills; six radiant springs
Danced over England in profusion wild
        Of luminous new leaf
Of myriad flowers starring the meadow grass
        Birds singing fierce and free,
Till the sixth autumn came, and brought conception . . .
In the first months of fifteen thirty-three
Came stirrings of a most determined child.

PART FOUR

15

Reader

Wyatt has long recovered from malaise,
Jesting and jousting with the best of them
Through merry summer days.
His lute no longer plaintive
But lively and attentive
Elaborates each phrase;
And other, kinder ladies,
Most notably, Bess Darell,
Receive a gentler praise.
Seeing his monarch daily
He walks the tightrope gaily
And conquers him at tennis
No wrath his heart dismays.

Wyatt

Yes, I recovered soon and was myself,
In that sweet perilous Anne no more delighting.
"Sometime I fled the fire that me brent
By sea, by land, by water and by wind"
That autumn I was writing.
"Lo! how desire is both sprung and spent
And he may see what whilom was so blind."
The King, unhappily, is still unseeing;
For him, as yet, no freeing
From his beloved bondage
To that wild being.

* * * *

Henry

This hard-fought battle
Over my marriage, still un-moving stood
Through all these years, and no advance was made:
None of my urgency did any good.

But at length,
A certain hope has beckoned
Of marriage buttressed by legality.
For if the Pope has consecrated Cranmer
To be Archbishop here,
He can proclaim the utter nullity
Of my first marriage, and perform my second!
The pathway can be clear.

Since each attempt miscarried
And for long years the mighty matter tarried,
It now seems crystal clear
That Charles the Emperor is supreme in Rome,
And this at last, in rage, I understand.
I will be master now in my own land,
Since Anne is now with child and must be married.

Henry

A Reformation Parliament is called,
Acts to restrain Appeals come thundering out—
No more recourse to Rome.
"By divers sundry old authentic histories
And chronicles, it is manifestly declared
This realm of England is an Empire . . .
Governed by one supreme head and king."

Here is a ruling that let no man flout!
Nor pettifogging clerk complain about.
My sovereignty's entire!
Here's history's true ring!

Is not this potent England? I'll proceed
To terrify the priests to acquiescence.
Lies, cunning, pressure, false humility—
No holds are barred.
If Popes are stony, I can be as hard—
Seizing the matter in my single hand,
Dragooning Council, and dragooning Commons
Until they understand.

Lonely and ill, Kate is still adamant,
Immune from practicality
Deaf as a post to need.
Women are kittle-cattle, who'll gainsay it?
Wedded so fast to conscience and to creed.

I turned to Cranmer: could he learn to play it?
And play it wholly legally, at speed?
For now, there is great need.

Since nature played a card, as is her way,
This fateful summer of fifteen thirty-three.
At length, last autumn
Anne had agreed to total consummation
And is with child by me.

Maurillac

"Si le ventre croiste tout sera gaté"
Observes the French Ambassador, with glee.

* * * *

Henry

So to the pendulum
Of hope and fear, intrigue and counterplay
Each passing month achieves a wilder swing
More urgency, each day.

Now Thomas Cranmer has been made Archbishop
Installed at Canterbury against his will.

Henry

Can he achieve in time the celebration
Of long sought marriage between me and Anne
        (Having dissolved our marriage)
Before arrival of the Papal ban
        And ex-communication?

        Luckily, as we know,
        Rome is a far off place;
But all the same it will be touch and go.

Wholly undignified, this kind of thing;
A game of tennis between Pope and King
With those pre-judging, worldly Cardinals
        Unfit to hold the ring.

* * * *

Reader

Meanwhile, the general murmuring against Anne
        Turns into exclamation—
        "She is a diabless!"
        "And a tigeresse!"
"Author of all the mischief in the realm."
But in despite of all recorded murmur,
All careful protest, even subtle sting,
Her charms continued still to overwhelm,
        Her grasp grew ever firmer
        On the besotted King.

Chapuys

        "He is by nature kind
        And generously inclined",
Wrote Chapuys to his master Charles the fifth;
        "But now this Anne
        Has so perverted him
        He seems a different man".

"Sir, his misfortune and his obstinacy
        Have closed his ears;
And something more than words will now be needed
        To move him", Chapuys pleaded.

Henry

"We are a body politic compact"
My reformation Parliament declared,
"And none may now appeal from here to Rome";
        Judgment now rests at home.

I told the Emperor's Ambassador
        Protesting at this matter,
        "I must have sons".

Chapuys

        "But would you?" Chapuys asked me,

Henry

        On what ground?
"Am I no man?" I thundered fiercely at him
"A man like other men?" As strong and sound?

Henry — He started on the argument anew
Of brother Arthur's dealing with his bride
Chapuys — Saying "their marriage was unconsummated".

Henry — But this was talk I hated,
"If ever I said Queen Catherine came as virgin
I said it as a jest" I told Chapuys,
As men, when feasting, utter words untrue.

The Emperor Charles, I said self-righteously,
Has never any right
To interfere, or make me live in sin,
As Catherine and I were never married
By canon law, and must not now begin
Once more, our life of ***sin***.

In January I'd married Anne Boleyn
In April Cranmer granted my divorce,
(A proper muddle, it became, all round).
By Easter, Anne was peacocking as Queen,
By Whitsun, she was crowned.

Six months before my love was brought to bed
We two, at last, were wed
With every splendour, every decoration—
And noticeable lack of acclamation
From the King's lieges gathered in the streets
And all along the gilded waterfront
And leaning from the houses overhead.

* * * *

Reader — Whitsun is forty days away from Easter
In which the public mood had time to change.
Nothing so ill succeeds as ill success—
Pity was swallowed in forgetfulness.

Catherine the while's forgot
By fickle crowds who used to mourn her lot.
They hear the bells, and see the banners quiver
On gilded barges, all along the river,
"Marvellous harmony of instruments
As of another world" the listeners said,
As the procession towards Westminster
Was grandly led.

Henry — Gold on the ripples, laughing, dancing, clowning,
The merry river turned to brilliancy
All sad remembrance drowning,
As Anne, from Greenwioch Palace, for her crowning
Was rowed, rejoicing, up the summer Thames
In a grand barge, with cloth of gold her dress,
While the guns roared salute . . .

Henry
And I, the splendid King,
Who'd decked her with the jewels and bridal ring,
Welcomed her home, clapped hands to her fair body
Already swelling with my daughter Bess.

Wyatt
Calmly resolved that even for flirtation
His time is up,
A cheerful Wyatt, at Anne's coronation,
Splendid in velvet, bears the golden cup.

Henry
The child's a girl, and therefore vulnerable.
I named her for my mother
Elizabeth of York.
But could not help remembering another
Most vulnerable heir,
And thought with pain
Of the boy King Edward and his younger brother,
My two young uncles, spirited away
By cruel traitors, never more to reign.

This must not come again.

For women, life is rough,
Short and uncertain under childbed's perils;
I must have sons. Two girls are not enough.

Reader
And now poor Mary is discredited
Princes of Europe will be slow to wed.

Henry
Although a girl, Elizabeth is ***mine***.
We christened her with an enormous state
At Greenwich, with a banquet of rich food,
A handsome flow of wine
And gorgeous robes, and generous revelry.

And as the autumn dusk
Rolled gently into dark,
And stars were seen through each September tree,
And lights pricked out along the Isle of Dogs,
Torchlight processions wound about the Park
And all through Greenwich village,
Their flaring gold reflected
In the dark river winding to the sea.

And yet, and yet,
For all of Anne's bright masquerades and routing
And the evening sounds of music over water,
Some part of me could feel, behind the shouting,
The bells that swing, the trumpets that rejoice,
Cold silence falling;
The fate of Catherine and of Thomas More;
The silence of irrevocable choice.

Henry

Night falls, as it must fall on every deed,
And sleep succeed.

But in the cold small hours
The mind will grow strange flowers.

Through the dark silence comes,
Distant, inconstant, unavoidable,
The thunder of the drums.

Through each to each is giver
Of mutual delight,
Along the calm bright river
More ominous than all
Though ever out of sight,
The roar of waterfall,

The far off smoke of foam
Bearing us far from home.

And turning in their sleep, the lovers shiver.

16

Henry

How soon the bells are silent, and the tides
Roll all the pageanty away to sea!
Red-haired Elizabeth is duly christened
But the deep longing for a son abides . . .

And Anne's dark eyes have learnt a sharper glancing;
She turns a termagant, and seeks to rule
Henry the ruler, tries to govern ***me***
With all the tyranny of her flesh entrancing.

Reader

Poor girl, between the Howards and the French court
She'd learnt in a hard school.

Henry

How light she danced! But there's an end of dancing.

Once settled as a wife, and lifted high
As Queen of England, this dark beauty proved
Proud and capricious; and her jewels gleamed
With no less hard a glitter
Than black and lustrous eyes
That now revealed the hidden greed within,
Fixed on me with insatiable demand
For lands, and wealth, titles for all her kin.

How far from all I'd dreamed—
Settled affection, matrimonial peace . . .

Henry

God's death! the fretful waywardness of Anne!
So often she'd decline
Life's casual happiness, be satisfied
With nothing and with no-one under Heaven!
Still her demands increase.

(Nor could I ever see
She might have learnt this way of life from me.)

Under these naggings, and the changing fancies
Of her eternal wearying caprice,
Desires emasculate . . .
How soon a burnt out passion turns to hate!

Through the long years we waited, that clear head
Hard as a diamond, was entirely set
Upon the Lord's Anointed
As husband and as useful instrument,
From whom she meant to get
All that there was of glory to be had.
But now, too bad,
Instead
Mistress triumphant turns wife disappointed.

There was no comfort, no serenity.
Love was awry, life had become disjointed.

Reader

Seized from her first love, Percy, by his will
Nothing in Anne can love him, or be tender.
Although she sweetly kissed
She only loved his splendour—
This thought his mighty egotism missed.

How sure love is, how sure . . .
Fooled by his passion, armoured in his pride
He thought her all of sweetness and allure.

Henry

But now her vixen rage
Has turned love surly, and drawn passion dry.
We were both wilful, and both little taught
In giving, although experts both in taking;
No longer even lukewarm our love-making.
There's nothing more distasteful or more loathly
Than that which once devouringly we sought.
Gentleness falls away, and even kindness—
And I am turned to stone.

Reader

And the bewitching woman left alone
To write her tragedy on history's page.

* * * *

Reader
Three months before her death
Queen Catherine, still a fighter,
Wrote to Pope Paul the Third to speak her mind,
Deploring Clement's impotence to right her,

Catherine
Saying she "knew not who to blame the most
Her husband or the Pope".
Dying of cancer, she would not say die,
Neither excuses for them both would find
Who had combined in different ways to slight her;

Reader
This pretty woman hardened to divorcée
And giving no-one rope.

Henry
Kate must be ever right:

Reader
Her obstinacy was like Margaret Thatcher's,
She's made of iron stuff.
In excellence of heart she did the damage,
And thereby demonstrated
That the best will in the world
That will not hear advice, is not enough.

Reader
Yet as her hour drew near
She softened, as so many do, well knowing
That whoso wants to live
A life eternal,
And find forgiveness from God's mercy flowing,
Must first, themselves, forgive.

And as her life grew nearer its completeness
She thought of Henry, and forgiving him,
Wrote him a letter of unchallenged sweetness.

Henry
Now, in a mournful manor at Kimbolton
Moated by my neglect, and by dark water
Near death Queen Catherine lies.
"Remember now the safeguard of your soul"
She begged me yet.
Far from a kindly love, and her dear daughter,
And from a lord who can so soon forget,
Free now from all disaster, all surprise
Still loving, and forgiving, always praying,
Aragon's daughter dies.

Her loving, like a lantern seen afar
Through a dark forest on a night of storm
Down the long years steadily beckoned me—
A light I would not see.

If there was now repentance, any grief
For that lost faithful love,
I stifled it. I felt immense relief;
This would at least
Stop Anne from teasing me to have her killed.

Henry

We ordered special food
And then sat down to dine
Dressed both in yellow, spent the night in dancing.
In this macabre enhancing
Of joint relief, did I reflect her mood
Or did she mirror mine?

Reader

Catherine's sad ladies murmur—"Poison . . . poison?"
As Spanish women will.
Her poisons were the desolate years apart.
There are few poisons near so sure and certain
As is the poison of a broken heart.

Henry

At times I'd wished her dead, but would not yet
Sanction the murder of a wife once loved.
That was to come.
Kate's innocence was like a fortress to her
Against that last assault of spite and scorn.
But neither could I mourn
Her payment of our universal debt.

In Europe, Emperor and Pope and Priest
And all who sought my overthrow and ruin,
Aimless at last, would feel their ardour chilled.
With no more injured Queen as vital weapon
Enmity might be stilled.

No more her skeleton will haunt my feast
Her weeping image hover by my bed.
That's over, and my marriage can be thorough
Unquestioned by the highest or the least.
No man can question the legitimate heirs
That I shall surely get in marriage bed
Now dutiful tenacious Kate is dead
(And properly interred at Peterborough).

* * * *

Henry

The child for whom Queen Kate was set aside
Is healthy and bright-eyed. To all she seemed
Keen-witted more than most, intelligent
Away beyond her very tender age.
Yet still a girl.
And I am not content.
Stubborn in love, and stubborn turning from it,
And stubborn for the sons of whom I've dreamed.

As the flesh fails in its intense allure
Anne's jealousies begin—
All other women leave her insecure.
Seeing my glance light on another woman
Anne underwent a shame she'll not endure;

Henry

And though I tried to soothe,
She, in a jealous fury
Miscarried of our son
Too long before his time
Losing the boy for whom I yearned so sore.

Reader

And so, poor stormy petrel, was undone.

Henry

Here was Anne's evening, here her last sun-setting.
"Madam", I told her, chill with disappointment,
"No more you'll have, no more of my begetting".

And a cold hatred, like a strong desire
Mounted within me, as I strode apart,
Feeling no particle of love, or pity

For all her loss, her sorrow, her alarm,
At this great horror.
Her anger, her hysterical caprice
Shuttered the feeling heart,
Years of frustrated lust,
Turned in me to ashamed and cruel disgust.

Men will invent their women to their liking;
And I invented Anne to please myself—
Her beauty, her enchantment, her devotion,
Even, perhaps, her guilt.
Her sins of mockery and of flirtation
Were real enough; and I have quite a notion
That that light hollow laughter at my verses
And my virility, she showed her friends
Are bitter, vile, betrayal.

There's the end:
My kingly honour was not built to bend.

17

Henry

There is no anger like the wrath of Kings
Who have been made unkingly by their craving.

That lovely, swan-necked Anne
Whose dark eyes glanced my manhood from my grasp
And slid it, helpless, into her slim hands—
She is past saving.

Reader

Too conscious of her power
Perhaps too proud to take the needful trouble,
She'd made no friends
To be insurance against the evil hour.
Few mourned the sudden drooping of this dark flower.

Henry

The people hated her. So now did I.
Only fools linger out the end of love.
Flicker of fire that does no more exist
Had better die.

Reader

Bred to ambition, Anne could not resist
Those velvet, rash, importunate young men
Haunting the Court when first she came among us.
Who played the lute, and offered love instead,
Kindness that in her loveless home was missing,
Who came, and smiled, and kissed
And turned to more than kissing.

Henry

Young Percy, and who knows how many other?
And these young merry rakehells served until
I was deliverance from her scheming uncles
And road to power within the marriage bed.

Reader

Kinsmen who pushed her on did not foresee
The rapid dangerous turning of her head.

Henry

And now, my purpose served
She ceased to love me. Even mocked my verse
With Smeaton, and her earlier paramours.
Mockery is the armour-piercing sword.

And mockery of me with other men
Worse infidelity than the act of love.
For this, for this alone she well deserved
Her pitiless reverse.

"Wild for to hold, though she seems tame"—
Wyatt had seen her clear.
She gathered teasing laughter round my name:
She was to learn, she was to learn in tears
Of wild, incredulous hysteria,
With courage alternating,
That there's no future safety in King—baiting,
That love's a perilous game.

Henry

I acted swiftly. As the day's jousting ended
Arrests began; and Rochford, Norris, Weston
Are hustled to the Tower
With its chill walls of stone,
There to be joined by Bruton, young Mark Smeaton,
And Wyatt, lodged alone.
Now, a surprised Queen Anne,
Trembling, awaits the hour.

A pliant Council sentence her to death.
The only mercy she received of me
Her kindly lord
On that extreme May morning

Henry

Was a skilled executioner from Calais
With a well-sharpened sword;
Who severed that long neck
In one clean blow, and made an instant end.
Anne was fastidious, and would have hated
A bungled job, making untidy wreck
Of so much elegance, and Queenly grace.
In this, in this at least, I stood her friend.
All her relations having turned against her,
Her uncle Norfolk, sitting at her trial
Condemned her, face to face;
Fearful for his own race.

Reader

Protesting innocence, they come to judgment
These so-called lovers of a fallen Queen.
Her brother Rochford, with a satrap mien
But an amusing tongue,
Condemned for incest; not a likely story,
Although he peacocked round in gorgeous clothes
And had a natural liking for vainglory.
Smeaton, who was too young,
And all the rest, who simply are good fellows
Who take their happiness where they can find it,
Brave men and no fit subjects for the gallows.

All are condemned, and sent for execution
Save only Wyatt.
All are beheaded, somethat hurriedly.
Did the judge fear a riot?

Were all these men too proud?
Their goods already forfeit,
None of them, on the scaffold, in extremis,
—Where no-one in this world can set them free
Or further punish them—None of these men
Cries out to the watching crowd
Lord, I am innocent and so is she!
But offer their submission to the King.
Here's a strange thing—
Unless their guilt was generally allowed.

* * * *

Henry

And what of Wyatt, what of faithful Tom?
Who told me truth, though I would not believe it.
So, at Anne's dispossession
When I beheaded all her earlier lovers
I spared Tom Wyatt—though he paid his tax.
Locked in the Tower, he saw his friend's procession
To early death beneath the pitiless axe—
Love's sharp and terrible end.
Friend, did I say? But kings can know no friend,
Kings such as I, stone deaf to intercession.

Reader — Tom Wyatt, the gallant courtier, yellow-haired.
Blue-eyed, and called "a man of wit and spirit",
"A comely fellow", and beloved of many
For charm, as well as merit,
"For well he knew to make and keep good cheer",
His conversation "of a merry fashion".

Henry — However true, he still is not immune
From anger or revenge for his old passion
That did my jealous rivalry incur.
He too, once played Anne's tune,
And even may have laughed at me with her.

Yes, he can watch in horror from the Tower
While one by one his fellow lovers fall
Under the vengeful axe.
Yes he can stand and see, grieving alone,
Waiting his hour;

Wyatt — Expecting every time, the gaoler's call,
The fatal footsteps nearing on the stone,
The priest, the blindfold, the untimely shriving—
Day after dreadful day.

Henry — He was her lover, he must suffer too
Before I free, but never quite forgive him,
Anne's sometime lover, with his feet of clay,

But truthful: so, unusually, surviving.

Wyatt — "These bloody days have broken my heart;
My lust, my youth did then depart
And blind desire of estate . . .

The Bell Tower showed me such a sight
That in my head sticks day and night,
There did I learn out of a grate
For all favour, glory or might,
That yet ***circa regna tonate***"

(I copied the refrain from Seneca
Writing of Phaedra, and her tragic fate.)
There's a strange comfort in recording things
That dulls the worst of stings.

Henry — This fighter, who's a feeling-hearted poet,
Had now to wait, and watch, and fear for life
As his friends die for coupling with my wife.

Reader — And there is many another man who would
Thus punish his wife's lovers, if he could—
Even suspected and unproven lovers.

Wyatt — So, for my own heart's ease, I write a ditty
For lost and erstwhile friends;

Wyatt

Possibly guilty, and yet never banished
From all compassionate love, or the stir of pity—
The orgulous but witty,
Rochford, the little loved, who highly stepped,
Norris, the dearly loved, whom many wept,
"Weston, Weston, that pleasant was and young,
In active things who might with thee compare?"
"Brewton farewell, as one that I least I knew",
Not known of many, but beloved of the few,
"Great was thy love with diverse, as I hear,
But common voice does not so sore thee rue
As other twain that doth before appear".

"Ah Mark, what moan should I for thee make more
Since that thy death thou has deserved best . . .
A rotten twig upon so high a tree
Hath slipped thy hold and thou art dead and gone."

"And thus farewell each one, in hearty wise,
The axe is home, your heads be in the stret.
The trickling tear doth fall so from my eyes
I scarce may write, my paper is so wet.
But what can help when death hath played his part
Though nature's course will thus lament and moan?
Leave sobs therefore, and every Christian heart
Pray for the souls of those be dead and gone . . . "

Reader

So sadder, wiser, sober,
And in his spirits decreased,
Though not in heart, Tom Wyatt is released.

Henry

Of course, I was not shown this latest piece,
But verse I love, and Wyatt is skilled to make it.
Passion for women, may the Devil take it!

Here is a man who is not to be wasted,
A skilled persuader, who has learnt his lesson.
I sent him to Madrid
And very well he did.

But in the living and the dying Anne
My happy pulses die;
And stony anger turns on any man
Daring to contradict me or deny
The rightness of the laws that I ordain,
Or my sole absolute supremacy.

Reader

Many men shuddered, at the Queen's swift fall,
Here and abroad. The Emperor and Pope,
Francis, and Pole, and Ferdinand, and all
Licked sanctimonious lips in satisfaction.

Henry

Shudder they might, but Anne was scarcely cold,
The last Carthusian had but barely died
Before the Emperor was on the ball
Offering Infanta Joan of Portugal
His niece, to be my third-time-lucky bride.

So much, so much for moral indignation!

Here's one imperial anticipation
        That is to be denied:
Never again I'll try co-habitation
        With an Iberian bride!
There's too much bigotry, and etiquette,
        And too much strait-laced pride!

Besides which, Spanish dress
        Gives me the shivers;
The blackness, the mantillas
        Convey to me distress;
My sharp antennae quivers
        At thought of such duress.

18

Anon
(*circa* 1520)

"The hunt is up, the hunt is up,
        And it is well-nigh day,
And Harry our King is gone hunting
        To bring his deer to bay.

The East is bright with morning light
        And darkness it is fled,
The merry horn wakes up the morn
        To leave his idle bed.

Behold the skies with golden dyes
        Are glowing all around,
The grass is green and so are the treen
        All laughing at the sound.

The horses snort to be at the sport,
        The dogs are running free,
The woods rejoice at the merry noise
        Of tantara teree!

The sun is glad to see us clad
        All in our lusty green,
And smiles in the sky as he rises high
        To see and to be seen.

Awake, all men, I say again,
        Be merry as you may
For Harry our King is gone hunting
        To bring his deer to bay."

Henry

All under the gold leaves of Savernak
Shot through with the September sun, unstirred
        By the still autumn air
Through paling bracken fronts I hunt the deer.
The home-bound rooks whirr from the harvest fields
The rutting buck runs startled from his lair.
        After long chase
        And long delirium
The stag his glory yields.

Quiet are the oaken lawns of Savernak
Boles of the beech stand grey.
Between the hawthorn thickets I pursue
        The sport that I adore,
        Through a long vigorous day
The sport whose pleasures are forever new.

Hunting is my obsession; a coercion
To further feats of speed and carelessness.
Horses die under me from huge exertion.
        They tire, but never I.
Never exhausted, never out of breath,
The lust of winning still absorbs me more
Than the strange passion for inflicting death.

His skill to my strong cunning, and his grace
        To my strong deed
        Yields in this sunlit place
Where after long pursuing dies the stag.
Reckless to folly in the hunting field
As in the tilting ground, I never flag;

Reader

        Acquiring, with his sport
Popular love; which fearlessness evokes
        More than perhaps it ought.

Henry

Pursuing also, down the grassy track
Old Seymour's dewy daughter. She indeed
May bring the gentleness and peace I need
        —After the storms of Anne—
        That in the lofty halls
Of all my draughty palaces I lack.

        How sweet is a fresh love
With its unconquered and undying hope
Falling upon a weary heart anew!
This is a girl with whom I think to wive
        —Small, fair, and twenty-five—
Honest, or so it seems, and chaste, and true.

Yes, Anne is still my wife, but why delay
While my mistrust curdles to certainty

Henry

And her determined downfall
Could happen any day?

Wolf Hall, and Jane's brave father, who is now
Ranger of Savernak Forest, knowing well
Its every beast and bird,
Each lawn and spreading tree;
And quiet old Lady Seymour, whose descent
Stems from King Edward Third.

Wolf Hall, and the silent daughter, moving quietly.
She guards some gracious secret in her soul
Where I could search forever, and not tire.
Something in her is absolute, and whole—
Jane whom I love, in whom I find repose
From guilt, from anger, from disquietude—
A spiritual rose.

That still pale face, those rustling silks, disclose
No enmities, no subtle small corruptions.
In that fair head no restless fancy grows.

Wolf Hall, and the many sparky Seymour sons—
Edward and Tom, who else?
It takes a while to master all their names.
Wolf Hall, and I as hungry; the bright flames
Leap in a generous hearth, the wine flows free.
The fire now glows around us, and we stretch
At else with exercise and plenteous food.
The clever and expressive Seymour faces
Delight me, an immense and lively brood—
Fully aware; but wise enough to wait
For the King's graces.

The St Maurs crossed the sea with Norman William
St Mauros went crusading,
Fought with the Black Prince in the fields of France,
Later, as Seymours, Bedford's battles aiding.

Such blood, and such a long inheritance
Can but the safety of the throne enhance.

Is Jane's a native grace,
Or was it all those tough exuberant brothers
From whom she learnt her place?

What is it all to me?
No more of this, no more.
I love her. I desire her. I am King.
The right true end of love
Shall come as surely as the racing sea
Rolls over level shore.

Henry

Desire is absolute; the only thing
That reigns in me, as I reign over men.
All this is clear—I love, and I am King.

Though Jane returns the store of gold I send
I'm master of more subtle ways of wooing.
        There can be but one end.

Wolf Hall, and a calm sense of certainty.
Old battered armour hanging on the walls
Sends back the torches' flare, and the fire's light.
        With a long serching look
        I know this must be right,
And call Jane back to Court; a quick decision
Which won't contribute much to Anne's delight.

Dear sister, and a well-beloved daughter,
        She's resolutely chaste,
Quietly refuses any furtive dealing,
Makes no concession to my urgent haste—
Whether from policy or honest feeling?

Some instinct warns me against pushing matters
        Over this delicate ground.

        Slowly, I bring her round.

        Made Queen, after Anne's death,
        How gently, undemandingly,
        About the palaces and terraces
        Jane's quiet presence flows;
        Mild as the summer's breath
She blooms in sweetness like a summer rose.

Untroubled by ambition, or by greed,
        Nor by the common need
To make herself important in men's eyes,
How graciously and like a Queen she goes!

My pursed lips widen, and those narrow eyes
That search men's hearts in dangerous surmise
Round into pleasure, and grow sometimes soft
        In sudden gentleness.
The stony will that holds men prisoner
In long and unendurable duress,
Under Jane's gaze, melts into suppleness.
The cockerel strut, that made of all my going
        A movement quite apart,
Turns to a casual walk: a strong forgiveness
        Plunders my iron heart.
Jane even begs me to be less contrary,
        And send for daughter Mary,

Henry

Which, when she's signed for my supremacy
(Looking the other way as she was signing),
I duly do;
And greet her with a kindness wholly new.

Nothing is sure. I might have turned away
Even from that serene and loving glance.
Would the long faithfulness of every day
Soon have become beyond my erring powers?
Could lasting happiness have come my way?

No-one can tell
We never had the chance.

"As gentle lady as I ever knew,
As fair a Queen as any in Christendom"
So wrote John Russell of my Seymour wife.
"The King has come from Hell and into Heaven
For gentleness in this
And cussedness and sadness in the other."

Men scorn the setting sun
To greet the rising moon,
But others who were well acquaint with Jane
Echoed the self-same tune—
From the Queen's tenants came a warm report,
Spontaneous, and untaught,
"Glad of her Grace as any heart can think".

Chapuys

But there was less ebullience from an envoy.
"Of middle height, and not thought beautiful"
Wrote Chapuys, rather crisply, to his Master
The embattled Emperor,
Still reeling from his Lutheran disaster
And not in any mood to welcome Jane.
Of new ideas, though less extreme than Anne.
Her general goodness and her prayers, did not
Impress the Emperor's man.

Henry

Some of the courtiers wrote her off as "milky".
Being all wine myself
I needed milk. And note
Milk is well-famed as poison's antidote.

Reader

Despite the deaths of Fisher and of More
Pope Paul was speaking with a gentler breath,
Thinking the trouble over, since Anne's death.
And with deliberation
He sought for Henry's turning to the fold
And the ending of his excommunication;
So also did the Emperor, and France.
Too many waves of doctrine had now rolled
Into King Henry's mind

Reader

And into people's hearts, and in the south
The new ways taken hold.
Henry's too happy with Supremacy
Clearly defined.

Henry

Also, we know too well
That when it comes to money, or to power,
Give Rome an inch and they will take an ell.

Reader

Yet he was hesitant
To swim along with the most radical tides
Of Lutheran and European voices;
Still heard the words of Colet, Fisher, More,
The tones of mild Erasmus, gentle Cranmer.
The total parting, so,
Reluctant on both sides.

Immediate danger tautened either party.
The Pilgrimage of Grace
With many varied motives
And both a civil and a religious face,
Brought many violent and treacherous days;
When almost all of the North
Passed judgement upon Henry and his ways.

19

Henry

Hunting and happiness,
Sweet talk, the warm caress.
But I must leave this land of milk and honey
To deal with that recurrent problem—money.

People want government but hate to pay.
There is inflation, people feel real hardship;
Complaints, demands increasing every day.

A Peasant

"Oure Englische nature cannot live by Rootes,
By water, herbys, or such beggarie baggage;
Give Englisshemen meate after their old usage
Beiff, mutton, veale, to chear their courage."

Henry

Incessant was the pressure—
Money for splendour, for security,
For Flemings, cash to subsidise the Dutch,
Money for soldiers, dockyards, and new galleys,
Money to build the tall enchanting palace
Men called None Such.
Money for colleges, and more for schools,
For gaudy garments for my followers,
For bells and hose for laughter-making fools.

Henry
Cromwell must see to it;
Its now the turn of monasteries to fall,
A process Cardinal Wolsey had begun
With those too inefficient, or too small,
Gutting them all
For funds to build his mighty Oxford College
To speed his mighty fame,
And (by the way)
"For the promotion of true Christian Knowledge".

Reader
Now, with those mighty, resonant foundations
Cromwell does just the same,
Making a monstrous mouthful of the matter
Making too clean a sweep.

Henry
There's need to cleanse the Church, but not to shatter.
My royal forbears had endowed them grandly
Now comes the time to reap.

Reader
Much nonsense was pronounced on sexual shame
In monks and nuns, which mostly went to prove
Too many were unfit for single life,
And should not have been there.
True, that a Yorkshire Canon has a wife,
Another several sons.
At Garadon, a fellow keeps ten boys
For pleasure, and another Prior keeps six,
And many priests have sons by married women,
And many nuns at Chester have by priests.
But human nature being as it is
Not all poor mortals learn to stay the course
Starved of love's feasts.

Clearly the system had become too slack,
Badly administered, corrupt in use,
Extracting too much cash from English pockets
And sending it abroad.
But that is no excuse
For giving ***every*** monastery the sack
For driving men away from the House of the Lord,
For cruelty, and despoiling,
Simply because
A greedy Cromwell wanted the money back.

Henry
Cromwell, you say? No, I!
Bankrupt by lavish Anne.
And so it was the mighty abbeys fell
Strong columns reaching up into the sky,
Arch after echoing arch
Beautiful with fantastic tracery
And gilding, and illuminated books;
Those grave and lovely aisles
Emptied, to win for me a wanton's smiles.

Henry

A frightened Council backed me to the hilt
The Commons bowed to my imperious will,
    Most of the rest kept still.

    Save a heroic few
Who contradicted rudely, and who knew
A faith secure and firmly disobedient,
    And a spirit
Beyond my power to torture and to kill.

Reader

Surely the way he treated the Carthusians
Was horrible, disgusting, and obscene,
Old Houghton and old Reynolds, and the brothers,
With courtiers even standing by to watch—
(Norfolk and Richmond were among the others).

This cutting down and ripping up alive
Though usual, is degrading and unclean.

Such men should be, like Fisher, "swiftly sworded",
    Cleanly and quickly dead.

Henry

It was my will. Reynolds should not have said
"Until the King be plucked up by the pate
And brought to pot . . . ".
Some matters are forgivable. Some not.

Reader

What matters are of moment? Hard to say
While they are happening on a normal day.
"Here are no news, the monasteries are down"
Writes their friend Husee to the Lisles in Calais,
A pious pair; and he himself no clown.

"No news." The many in this Catholic country
    Cared not so very greatly
    Which way the cat would jump
So long as they were certain to jump with it;
And not be numbered with the luckless rump
Sent to the stake as fervent Protestants
Or butchered for adherence to the Pope.
    Better to toe the line,
    Better to live,
Best to lie low and scramble for the lands,
    Better to wait, and give
Your powers of adaptation a full scope.

An age of faith is never without humbugs,
Never without fears and uncertainties;
Best to submerge your scruples, and survive,
Not as lopped limbs, or ashes in a ditch.
A faith exact has plenty going for it:
    More goes for being rich
    More still for being alive.

Reader

Faith too intense, too blindingly intent
On being sole, supreme,
Leads surely to the Thirty Years of War
As waged upon the blighted Continent
With cruelties so extreme
That Henry's efforts seem irrelevant.

Better, like those good Catholics, the Lisles,
To concentrate on adding Fristock Priory
To other goodies in your lawyer's files.

Henry

God, how acquisitive these nobles are!
And gentry too,
And so, indeed, am I,
Absorbing riches still.
We all want splendours, all want lavish living.
Hundreds of people feeding at our cost
And subject to our will.

Reader

But in the North, the greediness of Abbeys
Was less apparent than their charities,
Unlike the worldly South.
They succour men, and nurse,
And feed the hungry mouth,
And leave the poor sufficed.
It is from here the Pilgrimage of Grace
Will sally forth to fight beneath the banner
Bearing as legend—The Five Wounds of Christ.

Northern Woman

Old women who were ill
And paupers, felt the chill
Without the Holy Father.
The comfort born of sameness,
Of continuity
Is music to the old,
And the accustomed ways
More dear to them than gold.
All the alarms of change
Fill us with fears untold,
Times without Popes are strange,
Worlds without Popes are cold . . .

Reader

Yes, but we must admit
In entertaining nobles,
In catering to the great
The Abbeys are more bold,
Laid on the fuller tables.

Northern Man

By the Five Wounds of Christ
We will restore anew
The worship of Our Lady
One Shepherd and One Fold.

Northern Man — We'll free the King from evil Counsellors
And loosen Cromwell's hold.

Henry — Rebellion first came swelling out of Lincoln—
"Most brute and beastly of the English shires"
The King describes it crossly.
"How presumtuous are ye
Rude commons finding fault with your Prince!"
Suffolk must quell it quickly.

Suffolk — "Yes. But with what?" he naturally enquires.
We need a lot more forces to convince
That there is little future in rebellion
Against a stubborn prince.

Henry — A dangerous moment, and our men were few,
Entirely insufficient for the task
Of quelling rebels;
(Nor will I, ever, yield them what they ask).

Let them go home, and I will pardon them
And look at all their grievances anew,
I made old Norfolk promise Robert Aske
Their brave and honest leader.

Reader — And he belived this promise to be true,
He swore his fealty henceforth to the King
A promise never at this stage forgot.

Henry — A promise kept, exacted in such danger!
So I, of course did not.

Luck, as so often, held.
My dangerous Catholic foes
The Emperor and France
Who'd hoped just such a chance,
Were still employed in fighting one another.
And Turks were making trouble . . .
The guns along the Adriatic boomed.
Without Imperial help
The Pilgrimage of Grace was surely doomed.

Reader — Though there was outraged piety, religion
Was made the mask of many discontents
From brother warring steadily with brother.

Henry — Men hated Cromwell, were not false to me,
And all those doughty figures of the North
Dreaded encroachment;
From central power determined to be free.

Reader — Cranmer had now ordained the English Bible
And the Commandments, put in every church,
This seemed to the North intrusive and unfair;

Henry

They wanted Princess Mary
Acknowledged as my heir,
And the Pope re-instated.
Fate, and myself, would leave them in the lurch.

Rebellion broke anew.
Though now I was prepared
I feared the mighty North in such confusion.
Aske was now lording it at Pontefract
And with the foreigners was in collusion.

Reader

Full forty thousand yeoman under arms
Gave cause for great alarms.

Henry

William the Conqueror laid the North in waste
And here's my chance to give them all a taste
Of milder medicine, and to organise
This region full of striving lords and lordlings,
And lawlessness, and ambush, and surprise.

For feudal landlords I would substitute
More members for the Commons, better justice
Sternly enforced, to stop
Rape, murder, loot.

I drove a wedge, of course, between the rebels:
Repudiated promises I'd made
In time of weakness; brought in martial law,
And pulled the North together to be ruled
More fairly than they ever were before.
The rising was soon over, harshly punished
Through every rank and grade.

Reader

The poor, as usual, suffered to the hilt.
Before the scaffold, a long peasant line
Stretched out in mixed defiance and despair
Bewildered to be there.
Two hundred and sixteen were put to death.
And of the prouder sort
Constable, Darcy, Percy, and two Abbots,
Dammed in a summary court
Were all beheaded, and their limbs exposed
In towns from Trent to Tyne.

Henry

Brave Darcy quitted Cromwell with a shout
Of memorable prescience—

Darcy

"One remains
That shall strike off thy head!"

Henry

True words: for so in time it came about.
The hand that struck was mine.

Reader

And so the Dissolution trampled on
With heavy feet, and fear,

Reader
Over the monasteries, remote or near:
Houses dismantled, more monks driven forth.

Henry
And so also was founded for much good
The Council of the North.

Reader
Not all of this was suffering and woe.
Many an abbot changed to village parson
Or bishop; churchmen keep a lot of wealth;
And new schools grow.
And monks contentedly were pensioned off,
Many were pleased to go.
Not all the wealth
Raised up a middle class that through the years
Slowly absorbed the royal power by stealth.

Henry
As artist in the exercise of power
This confrontation and this settlement
Achieved my cruellest and my finest hour.

* * * *

Reader
Yes, we move mountains
Seeking to alter all things for the better.
But underneath, discover
The unexpected, unpredictable fountains
That swamp our best endeavour,
So, we become time's fool
Fortune's unwilling debtor.

Henry
They that are born as monarchs needs must rule.
Great matters are not always brought to birth
By those alert and strong, but its by such
That they must be concluded, forwarded,
By masters of the inexorable ''Must'',
Men who will not forsake
The purpose once embraced,
Seizers of chances that will make or break.

People are led to good and needful ends
Not by dear friends
But men who are not flawless but robust,
Able to master fear as to induce it,

Men who can say—You must.
Men who have temper and at times can lose it—
The Williams, Henrys, Edwards, Marlboroughs, Drakes,
Bringing great change to birth
—Though they had little notion to produce it—
The Wellingtons and Churchills of the earth.

Even such a one was I.
Not always clever, far from always good;
Too lazy, sometimes, to direct the rule,
But sure to give the reins to one who could.

20

Henry

At Greenwich, autumn passed in happiness
With this new love, this dear-beloved woman.

Reader

No thought disturbed him of the mourning north
For wife and child left starving,
For homeless driven forth,
Since those who should provide
Were blackened bodies swinging,
Were rebels who had died.

Henry

So perish all betrayers!
And all who speak untruly
Of laws that I may pass
(Always most carefully through Parliament)
Certain of good intent;
Certain as fate that I had acted duly,
I trod my way to Mass,
With conscience clear I said my daily prayers.

Jane

And we rejoiced, as always we rejoiced
In the calm passing of the silent river,
And the lights twinkling from the Isle of Dogs,
Great barges moving sea-ward on the tide,
Their brown reflected sails
Bending athwart the water's gleam and quiver.

Reader

The winter settled in an icy grip
Over the northern hills, the midland forests,
Over the plough, over the downland chalk.
Frozen the earth above the rebel bodies,
Frozen the corpse of Robert Aske in chains
Still hanging over York.

Henry

The Thames, this Christmas time, was frozen over.
Fur-robed, Queen Jane and I
Went down to Greenwich at a merry pace
From Westminster, over the shining ice,
Past the locked ships, the idle warehouses,
The frozen marshes under a pale sky.

Men moved with caution over the clotted ground
Of frozen rutted ways;
Silence, and whiteness, and a world spell-bound
Was broken only by our happy voices
And a soft hissing, as the runners race
Along the frozen tide.
The river sped beneath us, a faint colour
Glowed in her fair pale face.

Henry

And lower down the river, went ashore
        Taking to horses;
The houses stood white-roofed, and icicles
        —Those shining luminous spears—
Hung from the spars of many ships laid by,
Waiting in nakedness the distant thaw.

And so, our cloud of happiness would float
Above the winter and the frozen hills.
She danced to every tune that I would play,
        I gave, and she received.
Often she prayed for the country and its ills
Beseeching me to spare the monasteries,
        To stay the hand that kills;
She saved a nunnery from Cromwell's grasp.
And in that January of iron fields
And frosted forests lost in winter's sleep
        My wife conceived.

        New life of mine begun!
Is this the longed-for, ever hoped-for son?

* * * *

Wyatt

Sir Thomas Wyatt, writing from Madrid,
His Majesty's Ambassador to Spain,
The month of April, fifteen thirty-seven,
To his young son, new married. (Still to bid,
being but fifteen summers of his age.)

" . . . I have nothing to cry and call upon you for but honesty, honesty . . .

And here I call not honesty that men commonly call honesty, as reputation for riches, for authority, or some like thing, but that honesty that is wisdom, gentleness, desire to do good, friendliness, and truth above all the rest . . .

Venture not hardly by mine example upon naughty unthriftiness in trust of God's goodness, for besides the shame, I dare lay ten to one ye shall perish in the adventure . . . Make your example of wise and honest men; shoot at the mark . . . He shall be sure of shame that feeleth no grief in other men's shames. Have your friends in reverence and think unkindness to be the greatest offence . . .

Love well and agree with your wife, for where is noise and debate in the house, there is unquiet dwelling. And much more when it is in one bed. Frame well yourself to love, and rule well and honestly your wife as your fellow, and she shall love and reverence you as her head. Such as you are to her, so shall she be to you . . .

Remember that long life followeth them that reverence their fathers and elders. And the blessing of God for good agreement between the wife and husband is fruit of many

Wyatt

children, which I for the like thing do lack, and the fault is both in your mother and me but chiefly in your mother . . .

Seek not, I pray thee my son, that honesty which appeareth and is not indeed . . . Honesty is no common thing to come by: but so much it is the more goodly for that it is so rare and strange . . . A great part to have all these things (of goodness) is to desire to have them: and although Glory and honest name are not the very ends for which these things are to be followed, yet surely they must needs follow them, as light followeth fire, though it were kindled for warmth . . .

Consider a man's own self, what he is and wherefore he is. And herein let him think verily that so goodly a work as man is, for whom all other things were wrought, was not wrought but for goodly things . . . Never do that which within yourself you find a certain repining against . . . My son, for our Lord's love, keep well that repining . . .

Take this for conclusion and sum of all, that if God and his grace be not the foundation, neither can ye avoid evil nor judge well, nor do any good thing. Let him be foundation of all; will these things, desire them earnestly, and seek them of his hands and knowledge them to come of him . . . so liberal and good is he. I would fain see that my letters might work to frame you honest . . . "

Reader

Young Tom, a prankish fellow but good soldier
Died on the block in Mary Tudor's reign,
Having led seven thousand Kentish men
Not to dethrone her, but to stop her marriage
With Philip, Prince of Spain.
In trial, and in extremis on the scaffold
Young Tom absolved Princess Elizabeth
From any knowledge of his own rebellion:
Thus saving her, he perished not in vain.

Wyatt

So much of energy, so much clear purpose
Culled, in the rashness of impetuous youth!
Yet he obeyed.
My call and cry to you is honesty,
Honesty,
And, above all, the truth—
Through life itself be fatally gainsaid.

* * * *

Henry

Late in July the Duke of Richmond died
My bastard son who never could have reigned,
Henry FitzRoy, a pleasing handsome boy,
Whom nobody disdained,
Taken by cruel consumption.
I had been fond of him, and he was earnest
That I was capable of breeding sons.
But soon enough, the joys were in resumption.

Henry

Summer went by no less in joy unfeigned,
The masques, the dances, jousts, and river parties,
        All the sad memories were left to sink,
And I was also, like her country tenants
        In Wiltshire, Dorset, Hampshire,
"Glad of her Grace as any heart can think".

The golden summer passed, and brought October
With golden leaves still thick on every tree.
I would not lead the Council of the North
Now duly formed, and due to meet at York
Lest rumours of disaster at a distance
Should worry Jane or the child, with idle talk.
        And on St Edward's Eve
She fell into her long uneasy labour.

A son! A son! a lusty lively son!

Here was the goal of dogged long ambition
        A living healthy son!
Fair as the morning, turning to the breast
With vigour and with appetite like mine,
My love and hope in Jane in full fruition—
The dear continuation of my line
Of Norman William and Plantagenet!
Of fighting York and clever Lancaster,
Who may be, if God will, the greatest yet!

        At last, a lucky get.

We celebrate in ceaseless revelry
And ceremonial cheer to him, my pride,
While the wine flows in fountains down the streets
        And everybody greets
        This hopeful life begun.
We kneel in thankfulness for this dear son.
And though I spared her certain jubilations
—Devized by the ecstatic citizens
        For Jane's and my delight—
The rollicks stretched from daybreak into night.

And in my exultation I destroyed her
Giving her natal weakness no respite.

        On the sixth day

Reader

The childbed fever all her frame invaded,
Winning at length. Day after day she faded.
Fighting with all her quietness and strength
        On the twelfth day she died.

*   *   *   *

Henry

Grief's tyranny . . . how do men overcome it?
        Now I am set apart
In that harsh limbo of the stricken heart.

Loss drowns us in an emptiness forlorn
        Where nothing has a point,
And every energy arrives stillborn.
For three long days I shut myself away
From the futilities of consolation,
Not eating, and not drinking, never sleeping,
Fearing to waken to such cold dismay,
        Wholly alone to mourn.

The worst of grief is guilt, is the might have been—
Chances of goodness and of wisdom spilt.
So far as I was capable of guilt,
I felt it now.
Why when the boy was born was I so blind?
So carelessly rejoicing in the triumph,
Giving no proper thought to all her weakness
        And selfishly unkind?

        Only at length I roused
To see my little Edward cleanly cared for,
Well guarded and well served, and fitly housed.

Ah, if Jane had lived!
She was my harbour after tempest Anne
        My gentle resting place.
If Jane had lived and borne me further sons,
Even had lived to shield them into manhood
        And held me by her grace . . .
How bitterly the tide of loving runs . . .

If she had lived my fame would have been sure,
My happiness, my sons, and their succession.

How white she looked in death, how pale, how pure,
As if no mortal hands had ever touched her.
        And how shall I endure
Living without her, but by being harder
        To keep our son secure?

No other, no more women can suffice;
Now there is nothing left to me but fight
To hold the kingdom for a manly heir
        Bought at such bitter price.

Some of myself has gone from me forever
The last shred of my childhood innocence,

Henry

Some inner dreaming hope
Spontaneous, rosy, unaccountable.
Some hidden joy that is life's recompense.

* * * *

Henry

In its grim wonted way, life rolled along;
Dulling its bitterness by just a little.
And after evensong
I would go rowing, lonely on the river,
Loving the solitude, the exercise,
The water murmurs as I stroked along.
What thoughts inhabited my teeming mind
Were for myself alone;
My sometime tears were for no other eyes.

The dusk would deepen and the evening chimes
Rang from a score of steeples in the town
Above the water's whisper, and night's frown,
Above the quiet dipping of my oars;

And no man durst appoach me at such times.

PART FIVE

21

Reader

How can you understand
Who live in a safe land
In a safe epoch, with so few who blame
And fewer still who punish,
The urgency with which we staked our claim?

Disease and danger everywhere pursued us
Survival was the teeth and tail of the game.

At sea was likely shipwreck; and ashore
Were fires unstoppable, sharp deadly swords
Drawn without mercy, almost casually,
And pestilence
Most deadly, without cure,
Swept many hopefuls hence.

Simply to be alive
And grown to manhood, was a rare good fortune.
The harshness and exigience of the times
Offered no pardons;
A simple cut, a bad cold, could be fatal,
Death stalked the neo-natal
And seized on many mothers.
In such climes
Its no light effort to see men as brothers,
The frail heart falters and the strong heart hardens.

The man of peace
The gentle, the forgiving,
Many a time found here the shortest living;
The children die as dew
Dies in the summer sun
Their innocence and joyfulness devoured.
Only the hearty and the hale survive,
Only the lucky few
Live to be thirty-five.

Yet—which is more than you—
We all believed in God as a loving Father,
Man as immortal soul.
God as transcendent being, who would rather
We should not die, but flourish and be whole;
And comfortably think of him as Lord.
Comfort that many a soul with central heating
Cannot afford.

And though on earth our cries
And bitter protests fail,
Unheard our dying groan,

Reader

We look with confidence
Towards another country
As yet unseen, unknown,
Where souls were not for sale
A land where wrongs were righted
And God's sweet justice would at last prevail.

Judge if you dare
The snatching greed, the cruelty, the lust,
Of those whose cave of safety was so bare,
Whose lives sped fast,
Whose every minute well could be our last,
Who breathed a deadly poison
Even in city dust,
Whose chances of survival were so rare.

* * * *

One April morning of fifteen thirty-three
On a sad day
Had died Erasmus, peaceful and humane.
Now those twin tigers, Loyola and Calvin,
Rival extremists of the Christian faith
Are on their fiery way.

22

Henry

Now yearly my heart hardens
Yearly my sense of justice grows less nice,
Hopefulness mastered in gross appetite.
And any whose ambition threatens Edward
Must fall, by one or another grim device.

They must be ***killed***, any who threaten Edward,
And not imprisoned, later to emerge
And take revenge upon the innocent.
And spies must now be sent
To watch the movements of the traitor Pole,
My cousin, who aspires to papal role.

Reader

For full three weeks Queen Jane had lain in state,
Before her burial in St George's Windsor
In fullest ceremonial.
But mourning has to cease
Specially for lonely kings who need to carry
Burdens of state and matters matrimonial,
All of which now increase;
And above all, men say, they have to marry.

A number of advances now were made,
—Men suffer love, but do not suffer long—

Henry — Numerous fair princesses took my mind
Margaret of France, perhaps Louise of Guise,
Or Danish-born Christina of Milan?
There's Marie of Vendome; and of Lorraine
Their Countess Anne?

And naturally I want to see them first,
Prefer them to be mustered in a row.
But France declines to stage a Princess show;
Francis — Girls are not horses, mocking Francis said
To prance in a parade!
No progress made:
And soon, ***this*** matrimonial bubble burst.

Reader — A horse is what His Majesty receives
Just two years later, marrying Anne of Cleves,
Whom mocking courtiers call the Flanders mare.

* * * *

In Autumn of the year of thirty-seven
Sir Thomas Wyatt reporting to John Durley—

Wyatt — "The Emperor protests he will not meddle
(But to the good content of the King's will)
Between him and the Bishop of Rome.

Emperor Charles — "He'll do it of himself
With as great secretness as for his life"
Wrote Wyatt from Barbastra, by Mountzion.
"The Emperor understands the points of strife
Such as the Annates, and Indulgencies,
Exactions, Mediate power;
And with the Pope intends to justify
With reason, the King's doings;
To get King Henry's friendship,
—Not to hold him
In long suspense with discords and with jars—
To make the peace; with such result enduing
The King's successors with all benefits
The King himself has made,
Seeing that time itself makes alterations
And cannot be delayed."

Wyatt — Sweet words—but how much good will be ensuing?

Sir Thomas Wyatt to Lord Lisle at Calais.
In February 1538
"News we have none, but France and Spain be like
To make a truce until the month of June . . .
And of late

Wyatt

The Emperor departs towards Perpignan
To view the fortesses thereof and Salsas'',
And is returning soon.
''What we shall do then God only wotteth
And no man else. We stay at Barcelona.
Some reckon we shall go to Italy
And others to Castille.''
They say that ''Barbarossa[1] is at sea
And does much mischief in the archipelago
To all Venetian cities that there be.
I do commend your Lordship and good Lady
To the tuition of the Trinity.
Yours alway to command. Tho. Wiat.''

Henry

The Emperor—that ultra-canny fellow—
Was all for making peace
Between my Highness and the Bishop of Rome.
I would have no such thing:
And Wyatt told him that we English thought

Wyatt

''The error so discovered, that the people
Never would turn again to such a yoke,
Very much less the King.''

Charles

Then in his measured tones
Again the Emperor spoke—
''He that is sick may not be cured at once''.

Wyatt

Wyatt in answer, ''Sir, we feel not sick,
But rather of long sickness now made whole'',
In charge of our own soul.

Charles

The Emperor, as ever, diplomatic,
Said he would promise faithfully to serve
''The King my brother's turn, to my power''.

Wyatt

(But how soon will he swerve?)

And for King Henry's son
Whose life had just begun
The Emperor thought him come in a good hour.

Charles

''Was no less glad of him than of his own''
(Born ten days later on) he smoothly said
To listening Wyatt, who politely bowed.

Wyatt

The quarrel seemed as dead.

No word was spoken of Queen Catherine's wrong.

Charles

Although the Emperor said he would be glad
Had the new princeling been of his own blood,

[1] A Turkish sea captain with a red beard, whose approach was much dreaded by the Christian populations of the Mediterranean.

Charles
Yet he rejoiced as much
As had the boy been born
To Catherine, his aunt;
And prayed ''God send him a good life and long''.

Thus breathing his goodwill, reported Wyatt,

Charles
The Emperor laid his hand upon his breast
And swore it by his faith.
And so Sir Thomas took his leave and went.

Wyatt
We can surmise; but God alone knows best
How much the Emperor meant.

Reader
No major deal, it seems.
He has too many things to think about

Charles
—And much to much to do,
And vital undertakings
From Turkey to Peru.

Reader
Belief in Emperor Charles and his good faith
Is life in lands of dreams.

Wyatt
We still continue the negotiations
The never-ceasing nuptial argument
For joyless contracts between power and power,
In the interests of peace—
Henry to wed Christina of Milan
The Emperor's niece,
Mary to marry Charles's younger son
The Prince of Portugal.
They seek a monster dower
For making Mary wife to this young man—

Henry
Drive a hard bargain, Wyatt, if you can.

Reader
And what of Mary, all this weary while?
Mary, the unconsulted?

Henry
This hault Princess will do as she is told.
In any case
She'll have grown weary in her long exile.

Mary, I often dread,
With all those powerful cousins overseas
And an offended Pope to back her claims.
Even, a little, I fear Catharine
And her deep sorrow. I fear Catharine dead,
So blameless, unreproachful.
Her very goodness and forgiveness blames . . .
And may bring vengeance on young Edward's head.

Henry

Hissing and hatred from the Continent
Led by the new Pope, Paul,
Receive my innocent son.
And they repudiate his royalty
Deny his right to reign
And threaten me again.

Let them deny! I still defy them all.
Mary, forever Mary, is their cry.
Trouble is brewing.
They put her in grave jeopardy, so doing.
I guard her still more closely, in her exile.
Ought she, perhaps to die?

* * * *

Reader

Dangerous nights for Mary, Princess Mary,
Still slighted now as illegitimate.
Once the sole darling of her father's court
Her life may now be short.

Mary

Early night falling,
The dark and dangerous night
Rolling across the lonely countryside,
The lonely house, the house of hollow walls
The house of dripping rooves,
The shadows passing and the echoes calling . . .
And will the Emperor send to rescue her?
Is that the wind? Or sound of galloping hooves?

Another summer past.
Another autumn and the slow leaves falling . . .
The winter coming on
And will beheading, or some fate appalling
Come upon her at last?

Reader

The iron will stamp the fabric of her soul,
And the grim years that kept her from her mother.
Even the Emperor Charles, that canny cousin,
Told her to make the best terms that she could
And left her in the lurch.
So she had signed, looking the other way,
Her full submission to her exigent father
(Who once had seemed to her superb and good),
As head of the English Church.

Mary

She signed, with how much bitterness of heart
What spirit's death?
What conflict between duty and despair,
And fortitude and faith?

Reader

And then at length
They'd summoned her to court,
At kind Queen Jane's behest; and she had come
Biding her day,
Still, in her heart, looking the other way,
Though Henry had proclaimed her "his best treasure",
Still turning to the Continent, the stranger,
Still by her very heritage, a danger.

Now, a more hopeful heritage emerges
And if the money's right,
All the delight of a royal marriage,
If she consents, chance of a royal bed;
Mary may lift her heart to Portugal
And the throne nearest to her mother's home,
She may look straight ahead
Feel no necessity to glance aside
For ***there*** will be no threat of separation
From her heart's native habitat, in Rome.

Mary

I have not lost capacity for hope
That major Christian virtue,
But mine, now hammered into singleness
By long neglect and fear,
Is dangerously narrow in its scope.

* * * *

Wyatt

Sir Thomas Wyatt to King Henry's Grace
In summertime of fifteen thirty-eight
"The treaty of the first alliance, concerning
Th'Enfant of Portugall and your lady daughter,
They find the dote wonderous little, and say
It standeth not with the greatnesse
Of such a prince as is your Majestie . . .
Laughing, they named three hundred thousand crowns
But I suppose would be content with two . . . "

"In thother allyaunce concerning
Your royal person with the Duchess of Milan,
A hundred thousand crowns the Emperor gave her,
Besides fifteen in yearly rent of the Duchy
She has; and if Your Majesty conclude
Both these allyancies, the doary
Out of Milan, they note
Be taken in part of your dear daughter's dote."

Reader

Little financial rope
Wyatt has gained, for all his cheerful manner
His diplomatic using,
For little, in this matter of marriages,
The Emperor feels like losing.

Reader

Things are unpromising;
And Wyatt hurries home to ask for more,
Knocking without much benefit of hope
On Henry's iron door.

Wyatt

Sent back to duty, crisply, by King Henry
Who pleads "a time to think",
But really needing time for other plans,
"I was delayed by storms, the wind being great
And hath continued all this day till night,
So that no mariner would go abord,
Thus am I come too late".

But could not have come faster,
Catching the Emperor up at Barcelona
To find no mean disaster—
Deception very striking.
The truce between the powers, "Grandvela told me
Had been concluded", leaving England out.
"He promised that no mischief was intended,
But would not tell me what it was about."
The whole transaction "gives me grave misliking".

Do they suppose my master
Is not a Christian King?
Since he's denied obedience to the church
That rules in Rome?
Why do the powers leave us in the lurch?
For all the good of this particular mission
I could have stayed at home.

Reader

(One fact is not reported to King Henry
Of what the Duchess of Milan has said—
Namely Christina—she'd be well content to marry
With royal Harry
Were she two-headed, but she must decline
Politely but quite firmly,
Having a single head.)

* * * *

Henry

Traitors and spies are my adomination;
Monarchs should stick together
I told the Emperor Charles, when warning him
That Cousin Cardinal was on the way—
The traitor Pole, who would
"Pour forth the venom of his serpent nature",
And do our nascent friendship little good.

The Emperor is one superb fence-sitter,
Observing that he felt

Charles

"Cumbered between his conscience and his friend".

Henry

I give him little credit as peace-maker—
He only wants my money in the end.
Such indeterminacy leaves me bitter.

Everything's shilly-shally, hesitations.
Further enquiries for a wife in France
Reap but a crop of politic negations,
Of "frosty coldness", and of "slack remissness",
And that unlucky business
Concluded now at Nice and Aigues Mortes
For a crusade, formed against heresy,
Which, inexplicably, is aimed at me.

So, my attention turns towards the Rhine
    In hope to marry Mary
With Philip, who is County Palatine.
A comedown, from an Emperor or King
Where once I hoped for her destiny's fulfilling . . .
Philip is Protestant but very willing,
Mary must leave her pride of Aragon
    Castilian's high disdain;
The girl must marry, be content with children,
    Forego her ties with Spain.
Perhaps, at last, we shall achieve the thing.

* * * *

Wyatt

No go, again. Must we accept defeat?
My royal Master loves to cook in the kitchen
    But can he stand the heat?

Reader

The King is undiscouraged. Who's suggesting
    That he can not compete?

Henry

How comes it that our famous reputation
Around the Continent seem less than fair?
    Tant pis,
    I'll look elsewhere.

Nothing is doing here, nothing at all;
    But I am as I am,
    And confident to hang
    Rather as sheep than lamb,
Since my Ambition never has been small;

But still more sure never to hang at all.

* * * *

23

Henry

A King must be forever on the watch
        For the least change of look,
The subtle new inflection in the voice—
        We have no choice.
How many daggers hide in gaudy doublets
Silken, and jewel-hung, and velvet-slashed?
Behind the flattery, the bows, the smiles
        Unending danger broods.
What sudden treacherous moods
        Inflame the disappointed,
Those racing hearts wherein high hopes are dashed?

I hear that Reginald Pole, the chinless wonder,
With scanty beard and little sense of fun,
Cardinal Pole, who's named me as "King Nero"
Called me a "wild beast" and a "rotten member",
Is still abroad, plotting; the foul dissembler
Whom always I have treated as a son.
I had him educated; gave him treasure
        In valuable benefices,
Nor do I his rich pension still revoke,
        Was generous out of measure.
        Now he's turned enemy,
A snake to strike me, deadly in his stroke.

Because of their Plantagenet descent
He and his brothers put my son in danger.
With these intrigues their scaffold walk's begun.
One brother turns King's evidence, is cleared;
(Geoffrey, who'll walk the world a hated stranger),
He proves his brethren's loyalty is hollow.
Edmund, and Cousin Courtenay are both gone,
Lord Montague, the eldest, must now follow.

Reader

Even their mother, poor old Lady Salisbury,
Forfeits her life, as mother of this brood.
Daughter of perjured Clarence, and the last
        Living Plantagenet,
Past eighty, and unlikely to produce
        Further sons yet;
Mishandled by the executioner
Runs shrieking round the scaffold in her terror
        With head half loose.

Henry

She won't be spared. Mercy I can't afford:
All the Poles kept in touch with foes abroad
        And paid for their rash error.
I've not forgotten, and I never will
My two young uncles, boys of twelve and ten,

Henry

King Edward, and Prince Richard, Duke of York,
Seen playing on the greensward of the Tower
And happy at that hour—
Thereafter, seen no more.

Their splendid father dead, reft from their mother
By smiling men, the architects of power,
Tall men who made obeisance, and yet carry
These fair incipient monarchs to the Tower,
And bid them be at ease, and eat, and sleep,
Pending the Coronation,
And keep them there, still hopeful, unaware
Of midnight visits by the winding stair
Up which the deadly visitors will creep.

How long, ere they begin to be afraid?
Waiting at nightfall, with the leaping shadows
Falling on wall and floor.
Cold are the stony walls, and chill the space
Of stony floor that two young boys must pace,
High courage still displayed;
Two young Plantagenets
Well used to love and care
The royal and precious boys
Half fearless, half afraid.

High-hearted boys, unable to believe
How that most charming uncle can deceive,
That anyone could kill
Their royalty, or their sweet life devour.
Yet sometimes, in the twilight, trembling still.

Darkness at midnight over London Tower
And two young frightened children
Half waking, half asleep;
Noise of the town has faded into silence
The darkness grows more deep.
No sound, now, but their soft and final breathing,
And the slow opening of the turret door.

Even so, might die my boy.

Therefore, abolish all Plantagenets—
Anyone who might claim
Prince Edward's throne. Believe their treachery,
Since some of it is real.
Condemn the treason. Kill. Accept the blame.
One purpose. One conviction,
Powered by an icy Zeal.

* * * *

Reader

The Emperor's now at Nice
And Wyatt, still the envoy at his Court
Has little luck in his discoveries.
He knows the powers concoct a kind of peace—
But who's to be excluded?

Just to make matters worse
A jealous element is now intruded.
Bishop of London, Dr Edmund Bonner
Is added to the mission;
And constantly complains
In angry letters home—
That Wyatt has been no help in getting horses,
And in addition
The Emperor holds Wyatt in too much honour.

Bonner

Why won't he take us with him to the audience
"If truelie he entended to procede?"
"Wyatt rejoiceth when I do not speed
Lest speeding should become dispraise to him."
Why does he strive indeed
To get in touch with Pole,
With dubious John Mason in the role
Of go-between?
Is he in treaty with the Bishop of Rome?

Reader

A dangerous gleam settles in Bonner's eye.
Could Thomas Wyatt be
Imperial spy?

Wyatt

Seeking intelligence, wrote Thomas Wyatt,
"Continually I trotted up and down
That hell, through heat and stink . . . "

Reader

(Nice seems unpleasing to one Englishman.)

Wyatt

Where the French King, the Spanish Emperor,
"Pole also, practysing against the King",
"Bishop of Rome and all
Pretending to an union of the world!"

Reader

(Unlikely proposition, one would think.)

Wyatt

"Yet could I nothing hear, or make them listen
To the King's cause or benefit."
At Villa Franka so were our hopes hurled
And we were left in the cold;

Reader

Pushed off, you might say, from the back of a lorry.

Wyatt

"Cast out" the poet said "from a cart's arse".

Reader

Wyatt, the irrepressible,
Speaking one day of ribaldry, in jest;
And thereby courting from egregious Bonner
Some trouble of the best,
Leaving him sore and sorry.

24

Henry

Destruction of the shrine of Canterbury,
Blazing with jewels, a wonder of the world,
And seizure of the treasure of long years
Piled high, in dear devotion,
Finally caused my excommunication,
And left my cousin, Cardinal Pole, in tears.

Why leave this massive booty all unused?
And Becket? I've considered all along
Henry the Second right, and Becket wrong.
And long ago, when I was in my twenties,
Roundly asserted that a King of England
Has never had superior on earth.
He cannot be controlled from overseas.

Reader

All of which activates the Pope's decrees
Of fifteen thirty-five.
Strongly he feels
This is no time for lenience.
A Bull of Deprivation
Calls upon Christians everywhere to fight
And utterly destroy the English King
Whose subjects he absolves from all obedience,
(However great may be the inconvenience
To those who live in England.)

To active dwellers on the Continent
This ***fatwa*** has a fine resounding ring.

Henry

Imagine blaming me
For launching heresy!
Surely the angels wept!
I was as good a Catholic as ever stepped.

And not to be out-gunned by the chinless Pole
With his scant beard and his fanatic soul.

Faith is an ancient page,
Not closely studied in this hectic age.

Men live their lives in tightly closed compartments—
Faith in the holy men

Henry

Faith on the holy days,
On others, go as you please—
Desire, enjoy, and seize.

Faith with the courage to abandon all
That men perceive as most to be desired,
Faith constant, never tired,

Faith pure, entire, sublime,
Not as fanaticism, nor
As grudging doubt,
Faith beyond time
Exists; but there's not much of it about.

And this I dimly see,
While well aware that in this form extreme
Its not for me.

And the lip service paid
By all my royal cousins, and gainsaid
In every common deed
Where often they purloin
Land, treasure, lives, each ordinary wish
Of ordinary people,
To serve their need,
Such faith is not true coin.

Their lives and worship do not indicate
A license to dictate
To my intransigeance,
To my strong sense of what my people need,
Nor yet a license to invade my state.

Whence comes this poxy new conspiracy
From the joined powers of the Continent?
I was as good a Catholic as any,
And in my reign of nearly forty years
Burned but a single Papist, sent to the fire
Eighty-one Protestants (Though not so many
As did my daughter Mary, I admit,
Who burned three hundred in a brief three years).

Keenly believing transubstantiation,
Adhering to the Latin Mass entire,
Often confessed, I kept the fasts and feasts;
Every Good Friday I would creep to Jesus
And all through Lent I would refrain from meat,
Prostrate myself, at times, before God's feet—
Agree, a parcel of monks were sorted out,
And I was Pope myself, in choosing priests—
But, by Our Lady, whats the fuss about?

Reader

Enormous armies gather, it is said
(Though said with how much truth?)
The sentinels are set all round the coast,
And anxious, searching eyes
Quarter the narrow seas from Beachy Head,
Where sea-gulls swoop and cry
Over the turf of this beloved land,
And far below, the calm of summer seas
Sighs on a pebbled strand.

Henry

Berwick, Carlisle, Holy Island, Tynemouth,
And Hull, and Lynn, Yarmouth and Lowestoft also
Must now be far more strongly fortified,
With Aldborough, Orwell, Tilbury, Gravesend,
That all these Romish powers be defied;
The Downs, and Calshot, Portsmouth, Hampton Water,
Lyme, Plymouth, Falmouth, Fowey, Milford Haven—
Let none be left to chance;
As also Gisnes and Calais,
The only royal possessions left in France.

Now the invasion fleet is slowly gathered
At Antwerp, in the cause of Holy Church
To sweep my realm accurst.

"For that most pestilent idol, Bishop of Rome
Is minded now to rob and spoil the realm,
Inverting good religion" I declared.
But we shall see who cries 'Peccavi' first.

I built more fortresses, and coastal castles,
Reviewed the London levies, fifteen thousand,
Took promises for more;
I always have enjoyed a dash of peril.
"People are all, both gentlemen and others
Well-minded to defend their country here",
"They'll cast their ditches now, and stake the shore",
So ran reports the Council now received.

So far so good;
But Guelderland is vital
As counterpoise to thwart the Emperor,
And since her brother now inherits it—
Better be sure than sorry—back his title,
And bolster it by wedding Anne of Cleves.

Reader

Since France, Spain, Austria, Venice, Papal forces
Are all enlisted to achieve the goal
Once and for all, of dealing with King Henry
With his notorious headings and divorces,
Panic in some ensues—

Reader

Chewed into little pieces we shall be
        "A morsel between choppers!"
Tremblingly cries out Wriothesley,[1] P.C.,
        And Cardinal Pole
Is sent by the Pope to rally any stragglers
        And keep the Crusade whole.

Henry

        Though they accuse me wrongly
And have no holy cause to bring them here,
I'll fortify the country still more strongly,
        Strengthen the whole defences
        Stand, to the death, my ground.
Now at the serious threat of an invasion
        The angry trumpets sound,
And though they have doubtful affiliation
        To old, or to new faith,
Thousands of loyal yeoman rally round.

Reader

        This move was a mistake
        A major Papal error.
        Far from inducing terror
Threat of invasion hardens every heart.
Long grievances come springing to men's minds,
        Where there is planted, surely,
        An enmity to Rome.
This dress rehearsal for the Great Armada
Will only serve to make the Pope's task harder.

The King has no desire to break the Church,
But everybody wants to sort it out
        And clear it of abuses
Of some of the Faith's spectacular misuses.

        Monks, Henry said,
        Rather too sweepingly,

Henry — "Are an unthrifty sort of vicious persons".

Reader — But there was plenty to complain about,
Though nothing ruthlessly to put to rout.
Much of monastic life is worth its salt,
        But, when you come to look,
Is of itself now grinding to a halt.

And for the rest—the priests of homeless Christ
Who live in palaces and hunt like kings,
Employ their private armies of retainers,
        Are very richly fed,
        And over poor men spread
        Their predatory wings,
Are either lazy, or with varied others
        Spend too much time in bed.

[1] Pronounced—Rottesly, or sometimes Risely.

Reader	The priests who can't remember the Lord's Prayer,
The Paternoster,
And yet exact a fee for each attempt;
The clerks beyond the law
Whose sins, unpunished, serve but to augment
Their arrogant demeanors;
The randy Pardoner,
Peddling forgiveness round from door to door
As men will one day peddle vacuum cleaners;
The hated Summoner, who often comes
Demanding heavy sums
For one of fifty-seven
It may be, of Saint James the Lesser's thumbs—
Here is no way to lead poor men to Heaven,
More a conspiracy to catch them out.

No burial service before money down:
Even the candles, burning for the rite,
Are forfeit to the priest,
And all the dead man's clothes; yet for real sins
Remission may be had for half a crown,
Even for sins men have not yet committed—
A bonus for the wicked and quick-witted.

Henry	Don't the Pope's cheeks grow warm
With shame, at all those many centuries
When he refused reform?

Reader	Though hypocrite and bully
Effected Dissolution
Helped on by cunning greed,
And many a noble man was sacrificed,
For such a mighty cleansing there was need.
To many men it seemed
Truth had long died;
Most of the local miracles were tricks,
A priest-contrived illusion
To fool the simple, not to honour Christ.

Wyatt	"My call and cry to you is honesty
And above all, the truth"—
For this had not yet died.
And after all the hurly-burly's over,
The central truths abide.

Henry	Praise be to God, we have escaped invasion
And even Wriothesley can breathe again,
Here is relief and joy finding occasion!

Reader	Luckily Charles and Francis
Came quickly to their senses,
Or are perhaps impressed
By Henry's strong defences.

Reader
The Emperor decides
That Lutherans and Turks
Are more immediate foes;
France reckons the expenses
Of a cross-Channel venture
With all those racing tides
Make it too much to handle;
The game's not worth the candle,
And so the plan subsides.

Henry
"Kepe then the seas that are the walles of Englond
And then is England kept by Goddes hande."
This truism of thirteen forty-three
I was the first (of all who had the power),
To see the force of, and to understand.

Reader
Troublesome isle offshore,
Never inclined to turn the other cheek
Has had a narrow squeek—
And doubtless, in due season, will have more.

25

Merchant Seamen
Now look we for much trade
In oranges and wine, and well-wrought leather
Within The Emperor's wide and rich domain
The Netherlands and Spain,
Since this good peace is made.

Wyatt
Beware the restless weather
Of the Imperial will.
Europe's the steamy kitchen
Whose brew is rarely still.

Merchants
But many a luscious meal may there be cooked.

Wyatt
Tred softly, doughty merchants,
Lest you yourselves be cooked.
About the parts of Spain
Are mortal dangers you have overlooked.

Merchants
Tackle the Emperor once again, we pray you
Master Ambassador, on our behalf,
And do us this much grace . . .
We seek no martyrdom in cruel Toledo
Auto-da-fé in the burning market-place.
Nor do desire to sail home empty-handed
As prodigals who lack the fatted calf.

Sir Thomas Wyatt to the King from Paris
On January the 7th of 1540

Wyatt

"Please it, your Majestic, to be advertized . . .
. . . Further, I spoke the Emperor as touching
Evil entreating by the Inquisition
Of Englische merchaunts that are traffiquing
In your countrys of Spayne."

Emperor Charles

"He answered—the authority of the Inquisition
Depended not on hym.
It hath been stablished in his realms and countrys
For goodly reasons that he woll not breke,
No, not for his grandam's sake.
And any that will live in his countreys
Must live, as they live there."

Wyatt

"Then quod I
Whilst I was in Spayne it was promised
And then so used, that no extremity
To friendly merchaunts
Should be there showed . . .
The difference alone
Is different thinking about the Bishop of Rome.
It was thought reasonable
That no such rigour should be there allowed."

Emperor

"It maybe", quod the Emperor, "that they have done.
I will write soon to the Cardinal of Toledo
That I may be informed."

Wyatt

"Nay sir, quod I, for this is ex officio.
They trouble our nation; having it that tho
A man live never so uprightly
But by examinacions they sholl trap hym,
Where is no publication of witnessis."

Emperor

"I cannot tell yow . . . I shall wryte to Spain."
And then he answered
"The Kynge is of one opinion,
And I am of another . . .
I will not alter my Inquisition.
And if I thought they would be negligent
I would soon put them out, and then
Put other in their room."

Wyatt

"Sir, quod I, I come not to dispute. I am not lernid . . .
This takes away the traffique between merchaintes
Both yours and ours.
Shall we in this loke then for no redresse?"

Emperor

"Here, at a little, he stayed.
I will wryte, quod he."

Wyatt

"Be my trowth, quod I, the King can do
No more than to make knone to all his subjects
As manie as will traffique into Spayne
Do it at their aventure, since the powre
Dependeth on his adversary, enemy,
The Bishop of Rome,
And not upon your Majestie;
Against the wich
Tretys betwene you and hym shull be no warrant."

Emperor

"In that, quod he, the Kinge may do as he please."

Wyatt

"Why it is altered thus, I cannot tell.
If men set hand in other men's Goddes
There may be quarrels picked for that enough.
I know well that the merchaunts have been warned
Neither to teache nor do
Things contrary to the customes of your country,
And there should no man meddle with them then.
. . . But there is yet more, Sir, quod I
Prechers be sett forth that diffame the Kyng
And nation, and provoke your men agaynst us."

Emperor

"As in that, Quod he, prechers will speke
Against myself when there is cause.
And that cannot be hindered."

Wyatt

"Why sir, quod I, yourself have ere this
Commanded other ways
When I was in Toledo in like case."

Emperor

"I'll tell yow, Monsieur L'Ambassadeur,
Kynges be not kinges of tonges.
If men give cause to be so spoken of
They will be spoken of;
There is no remedy."

Wyatt

"I stood at this; advised him earnestly.
He made some countenance,
As if he would have been at a point.
Sayd he would wryte unto your Hyghness . . .
And so, he took his leave. And we came home."

"I saw in this access to the Emperour
That vehemence I have not sene bifor.
I note his louder voice, a look more earnest
In the imperious fashion of his wordes
In all this matter of the Inquisition."

"In the same points I heretofore have seen him
Far cooler, and more tractable,
Conformable to reason.

Wyatt

He feareth lest your majestie
Join with the Almayne
Whereby he may be hindered there.
And hath the meanes to shew you like displeasure
By evil handling of your subjects,
And shewing himself assured of these Frenchmen,
As you by joining Allmaynes and Gueldres
Do shew to him."

"To this, I think, pertaynes
Round words he giveth me . . .
And since your just withdrawing
From the tyrany of Rome
He thinks your bond of friendship
Shows no equality."

"But,
With power to treat and roundly to conclude
Methink we should soon drive him
So to discover himself . . .
And Our Lord have you in his blessid keeping."

* * * *

Reader

Wyatt is disillusioned over Europe
Does ***everybody*** cheat?

Wyatt

The Turks who slay their prisoners of war,
"Venetians who sow cockles[1] in clean wheat",
The Emperor, susceptible to weather
Blowing across the Alps or Pyrenees
Can never hold his course two days together,
Wheeling with every breeze.
"With good and gentil manners we parted frendes"
Wyatt wrote home;
Next day the alliance ends.

And as for France, that foxy, cunning people,
Nothing is at it seems;
One week as friends, the next
"Cold as though those things past had been but dreams".
"Th'Ambassador of France
Makes here soure countenance."
Playing a sorry game.
The young, the old, the middle-aged, the elder
All bloody continentals are the same,
"Cleves, and the Almaines, and the men of Gueldre".

[1] Corn-cockles—a purple-flowered weed, Agrostemma Githago.

Wyatt

"And I", Wyatt re-emphasized the point
"I, as God judge me", when at Villa Franka
"Continually imagining how I might
Do the best service" of intelligence,
Rested not day nor night,
"Trotted continaully up and down
    That hell and stink
From Councellore to Embassator, from frende to frende",
    Nor could get any knowledge
    Of what these powers intend . . .
Emperor, King of France, and Bishop of Rome
    (My Master's mortal enemy)
    Assembled to some purpose
"Pretending to an union of the world"—
Affording me no clue to what they think.

    And here's a piece of work—
    The French collaborate
As is their wont, with the invading Turk
    Who threatens all of Christendom,
And all this havoc Francis would create
Simply through envy of the Emperor
Whose power is so great
    And wider far his range.

Reader

    Nations don't change.

    Wyatt is now for home—

Wyatt

"Tagus farewell! that westward with thy streams
Turns up the grains of gold already tried,
With spur and sail I go to seek the Thames . . .
My King, my Country, alone for whom I live,
Of mighty love, the wings for this me give."

Farewell, just now, to Continental strife,
    Hail Allington, and Kent!

    And Mistress Darell, Bess,
    A woman born to bless
With whom I've lived long while as man and wife.

Reader

Nothing so happy lasts for very long
And men who serve the King must take their chance.
Too soon he's made Ambassador to France.

And so poor Princess Mary's marriages
To Portugal, or the Palatinate;
Wrecked on the shallows of her father's meanness
Are set aside without a backward glance.

26

Henry — Now, to my marriage matter.
Better be sure than sorry. We will send
The artist Holbein to portray both sisters
Anne and Amelia, candidates of Cleves.
Anne has the milder face,
Cromwell has stronger reasons up his sleeves.
And he insists that she is beautiful,

Cromwell — "Excelling more the Duchess of Milan
Than does the sun the moon!"

Henry — This seems to fit the case—
She must be sent for soon.

Reader — Wotton reports that Anne is not well-read,
Can't sing, Can't play a single instrument,
She isn't cheerful, nor can she be funny;
Chiefly, she likes to sew.

She's altogether very far from glistening
As royal ladies go.

Sadly, no-one is listening
To Wotton's wise defiance,
For Henry loves the portrait much too well,
And Cromwell loves the alliance.

Henry — Anne came to Canterbury, in cold mid-winter
After a shocking crossing,
The North Sea in a paroxysm of tossing.
I brought her down a present of rich fur
A cloak of deepest sable
Expressly cut for her.

Reader — But seeing Anne, he sadly said (aside)

Henry — "I am ashamed for I shall not be able . . .
I am unfitted . . . "
To mate with anyone so very plain.

Holbein was being simple—
Why did he paint her smoothly-cheeked and pretty
When anyone can see she's small-pox pitted?

Reader — No fault of hers, and may she be acquitted.

Henry — I greeted her with dignity and kindness
And we were duly wed.
What can't be cured must surely be endured.
We bowed, we kissed each other, went to bed
All to no purpose;
Nothing there occurred.

Henry

"Cromwell", I then protested
"I cannot be provoked by her, nor stirred
To do that act . . .
Though able well to do it with another".
There's the plain fact,
There's the unvarnished fact.

A pug-faced lady; and, as all admitted
Fatally small-pox pitted;
And, worst of all, she has "displeasant aires".
To friends I called her "one of Flanders' mares".
The men who lied to me will not be pitied.

This stupid plan will make the Dutchmen blame me
When I have need of them to be suborned
Out of the Emperor's power.
And what about Anne's brother, Duke of Cleves?
Nobody likes to see their sister scorned.

Cromwell

Without them, we shall still be isolated,
Prey to a disaffected continent
Full of enormous armies.

Henry

Be that as it may.
However great the harm is
This marriage never will be consummated.
Cromwell! What ***did*** you think?
You can take a horse a dozen times to the water
But you cannot make him drink.

Reader

This is a classic mishap
An error to appal—
So who will take the rap
And who will go to the wall?

Henry

The new queen must indeed be fairly dowered,
Though left a maiden. Richmond, Bletchingly,
Estates and retinues and waiting women,
To cushion such a fall.

Reader

Queen Anne, contented, bought herself new dresses,
And though her brother of Cleves
Pressed her to hasten home,
Anne would not hear of it
To her, the occasion was no time for tears.

For many sunny years
She breathed her bad breath happily at Richmond,
She liked her life in England, seemed to fit . . .
Long after all the rest had gone to heaven
Anne basked along, till fifteen fifty-seven.

Henry
Good luck to Anne of Cleves,
Who had the sense to take things on the chin
Where Catharine and Boleyn did not begin!
And we will stay good friends.

Reader
Woe to the powerful statesman who deceives
A lustful, choosey, hopeful royal master!

Henry
Come. Thomas Cromwell, come!
The most responsible for this disaster—
You may be churchman, but you are as well
Man of the world, quick-eared to hear confession.
Good manners and good sense are not enough;
Did you imagine I could bear to love
That sad-faced German lady, Anne of Cleves?
Policy can become too great obsession.

A King, as well as other men, believes
In making clever marriages for reasons
Other than sudden love;
But those ideas are treasons
That seek to mate a middle-aged sharp fellow
Made nice by many spoils
To maids as charmless as this short-necked woman
Who's endlessly pre-occupied in sewing?
This was as stupid as it was unkind.

Reader
Seeing the way the baffled will was blowing
Cromwell, no fool, now sought to make amends.

Henry
Yes, treat her well, for sure,
As far as money goes (which you must find).
Do you remember, cunning Thomas Cromwell.
(My most efficient, ever-working servant)
I married first, for policy and pride,
A luckless lady out of Aragon.
Small good it did, either to her or me
Or Christendom in general. Do not ask
The faithful martyred Protestants who died
Burned at the stake, nearly three hundred strong,
Our ruthless daughter's victims in three years
What ***they*** think of such pride?
And do not ask
A multitude of blameless Catholics
Suffering from Mary's wickedness so long,
(Four hundred years of hatred and suspicion)
What ***they*** have reaped from policy and pride.

* * * *

Henry
Cromwell enriched me with some further millions
Wrenched from the Commons and the Convocations,

Henry

And frankly plundered from the Knights of St John;
My lavish life went on,
While Anne continued to acquire new dresses.

Cromwell

If I felt sore, I smothered my distresses.
Meanwhile, ***my*** schemes with foreigners went on
Though at a different shop.
Once one starts scheming, and enjoying power
Its difficult to stop.

Henry

He's made a fool of me before the world
And will not be forgiven.
Soon will that proud ambitious soul be riven
When I have squeezed from him the final drop.

Yet I conceal a smouldering sense of outrage
Behind pacific looks
A pause ensured, in which I licked my wounds
Or buried them in suffocating pride;
And went on hunting, building colleges,
Furbishing Eton, likewise Westminster,
Listened to music, bought a lot more books—

Then came a turn of the tide.

27

Reader

Sir Thomas Wyatt is knee-deep in debt,
Since an ambassador by no means yet
Commands a salary from royal employer.
But, ever hopeful, he may yet withstand
That deeply hateful course—sale of his land.

Wyatt

"I woud trust
Littel and littil to creep owt of dett."
Aware of getting nowhere, cramped by lack,
He longs for home, despairs of continentals
And slowly comes to see things in the black—
"Men nowadays set forward all their matters
Wondrously with false rumours and with noises".
And in the Emperor's train he treads a quagmire—
"Things pass as much by looks as by the facts".

And since "the coming of the King of the Romans"
—Ferdinand, who's Archduke of Austria—
"Meeting with France waxeth cold and ever colder
Each day, and in the legate's entertainment
I see no great affection, nor great matters
In treating", Whether he's quiet or bolder.

Wyatt

In short, no warmth of greeting;
All converse hollow.
"Between the Almayne Protestants and the Emperor
Accord will shortly follow",
Expected any day.
As to the French, "the Almaynes scant believe
Whatever they may say".

And here at Ghent there seems a general absence
Of sweetness or of light;
Icy politeness at the very best.
Holden to Rome King Henry may not be;
And seeing this at length, the papist powers
Have lost all interest
In keeping in
With this outlandish monarch of the West.

"The Gauntois bring this day their privileges . . . "
And little of redress would come their way
From an exasperated Emperor, Wyatt told Henry.
All said is froth and foam
"I am not so necessary here . . . and by sides that
My money is gone . . . At Gaunt this Palme Sunday".
And he besought the King to call him home.

Answer came slowly.
Wyatt waited daily . . . and was told at length
There would be no release.

He felt his ineffectiveness increase.
"In all the movings of the Emperor
There's never certainty of where he goes
Until his foot be in the stirrup . . .
He takes occasions as they offer."
So why must Wyatt linger
The butt of every continental scoffer
When an urbane and diplomatic scorn
Greets all suggestion that he tries to offer?

Reader

He is a loyal servant all the same
And stays where he is bidden.
Whatever Bishop Bonner plans the while
Remains securely hidden.

Wyatt

"Would God I was as able as suffisance
As the King thinks of me" Wyatt exclaims,
"I then wuld never plain
Of this long waste of all my private things",
Nor think it pain.
"I shall persever in my duty.
It is no patience but a pleasure
To do the King this service . . . "

Reader

What the King thinks of Wyatt may not be known:
Henry's long practice is to think alone.

And though responsibility never ceases
Pain in his leg continually increases.

And has he now forgiven daring Thomas
        His love for Anne Boleyn?
Or does that steely jealously abide
An ache from the old wound to sexual pride—
Resentment dwelling deeply still within
        Waiting its lucky tide?

How will outspoken Thomas long survive
The sometime smiles, between the bouts of pain
In stricken Henry; how will he placate
By laughter and good fellowship, and music,
The snarling angers of the dying lion
        Flexing his claws again?
        How live through terror's reign?

* * * *

Reader

        Just now, the pressure's off—
Francis and Charles have fallen out again
Having no eye to "the quiet of Christendom":
        So Henry will complain.

Henry

So I've no further need of German soldiers
        And anyway, "at sea
        Germans are always sick".
Nor do I care to join myself with rebels
        Against their rightful lord,
With Lutherans, and heretics, and such
Uncertain quantities as are the Dutch.
And now that Cromwell's made a fool of me
        Cromwell will get the stick;
And I'll survive, my armour being thick.

        Now, it appears,
These unseen ladies of the Continent
Are not a needful marriage obligation;
        And so, made wise,
        I'll trust to my own eyes
Cast upon charmers of my native nation.

Reader

Resilient spirits soared
Within King Henry's breast
When Norfolk introduced his youthful niece—

Henry

Called Catherine Howard, lively and hazel-eyed,
Just twenty, redbrown-haired, still plump with youth—
She bowled me over. That surprising joy

Henry
Ran through me like a river, I believed
In every promise of those smiling lips;
And that's the truth.

Reader
Joy bubbles swiftly in an ageing man
Faced with a pretty girl; and there is always
The darling, cheating hope
That the enchantress will reciprocate.
The words unknown to sexual optimists
The words they will not utter are—too late.

Henry
Why, when the heart's as youthful as of old
Must love lie cold?
Age is in spirit; not in tedious letter;

Reader
And so this lovely she
Too young to know much better,
Pushed on by Norfolk, and her family
Is more than willing to become his bride.

Lord Edmund Howard, her father,
Has wandered off, a classic neer-do-weel,
And Catherine had been brought up by the Duchess,
Norfolk's repellent second wife, or rather
Neglected and debauched. They send a letter
Declaring her in all ways suitable
To wed a King.

Henry
Proudly and hopefully I place the ring,
A lucky man who could not have done better.

* * * *

Henry
Cromwell, the Norfolk faction won't abide,
And I no longer need
Since he's set up so fine an instrument
Of government by Privy Councillors
Under my will and guidance to proceed.

Reader
And so, this master of administration
(Maybe the best that England ever had),
Is for the drop.

Henry
Well, he has had a fine run for his money
A full allowance of life's milk and honey
Of goods and lands and wealth.
Everything has to stop.

Charged with embezzlement and heresy
''Mercye'' he cries me, ''mercye?'', from the Tower.
He has had his hour:
And how much mercy all this while showed he?
Few are the tears now shed at Tyburn gallows
At ebb of so tyrannical a flood.

Surrey

''Now is the foul churl dead'' reported Surrey
''Who so ambitious was of other's blood''.

Reader

Wyatt alone is deeply moved to tears
(Seen and reported by a Spanish stranger).
To see this old friend pay the price of power.
Cromwell, who saw him weep
And realized the danger
Involved in this display of sympathy,
Cried out for Wyatt's protection
(For his shrewd eyes could see
Spies in the gaping crowd
Ready to do him dirt)
''Ah Wyatt, do not weep,
Were I not now more guilty than thou wert
When men took thee imprisoned to the Tower
I should not now be in this pass''.
And so
Selfless at last in his most terrible hour,
With this intelligent gesture of absolution
Of Wyatt, from complicity in guilt,
Did Thomas Cromwell pass to execution.

Only God knows the whole
Of what lies deep in anybody's soul
Under the iron crust
Under the shabby, creeping, convolution.

* * * *

Reader

In France they shrugged their shoulders in disbelief.
There could be no worse war, the sages said,
Than that the English wage upon each other.
And while they war, no Frenchman will be dead:
Much thanks, for this relief.

* * * *

Reader

Henry proceeds in glee,
Looks ten years younger than he used to be.
The masques and dances glitter in due procession,
And Catherine kindly asks Queen Anne to dine—
Party ***à trois***—and yet it feels like fun . . .

Henry

All this may even mean another son!
Another son to strengthen the succession!

Reader

The sanguine soul rejoices. But in fact
It means another tragedy begun.

PART SIX

28

Reader

Our lord the King is steeped in fantasy—
He wears illusion like a warrior's armour,
Believing that the basest deed on earth
Cannot defile him.
And even on the scaffold, in extremis
His victims don't revile him.

So the charmed life of this conviction holds him;
His conscience lies asleep.
Only a vibrant wariness remains,
And an insatiate greed
For more ill-gotten gains,
Suspicion running riot
Swoops upon even the steadfast and the faithful—
Ambassadors like Wallop, and like Wyatt.

Henry

Suspicion swelled within me like a growth,
A haunt, an infestation—
Disease that knows no halting and no sloth.
Suddenly even Wyatt, and old Wallop,
"The King's most faithful servants", were arrested
And marched in chains to the Tower.
Such doings made men nervous
Their frightened spirits vexed.
Here is the reign of terror—
Who knows who will be next?

Reader

Everyone was astonished; and wrote Marillac
The French Ambassador in London,

Marillac

"Sire,
Last night, by order of the King
Two much esteemed gentlemen of his Court
Were taken prisoners, and this morning seen
With their hands bound, taken by twenty archers
To the great Tower of London, there detained.
. . . This Master Wyatt seemed
As much in favour with the King his master
As any great lord in the country;
There was no-one
With whom the King had been more intimate,
To whom he had given greater signs of love . . .
It is the third time that this Wyatt has been there
(Doubtless will be the last)."

"And he is more regretted
Than any man arrested
In England these three years,
By Englishmen and foreigners alike.

Marillac

And yet is no-one bold enough to speak
On his behalf,
So great are all mens' fears.''

Wyatt

Wyatt to Francis Bryan, from the Tower
''Syghes are my food, drynke are my teares
Clynkinge of fetters such musycke would crave,
Stynke and close ayre away my lyf wears.
Innocencie is all the hope I have . . .
Sure I am, Brian, this wounde shall heale agayne,
But yet, alas, the scarre shall styll remayne.''
Waiting, and hoping, and sometimes despairing,
Dark fates anticipating,
Remembering other times,
Having the feeling of a world uncaring—
Wyatt must wait, and wait, and go on waiting.

* * * *

Reader

In time he learned
That Bishop Bonner has prepared the charges,
Bishop of London and Ambassador;
Bonner, the sunny fellow, who once burned
Makins, a Protestant boy of just fifteen
To whom he'd promised pardon on repentance;

A charmless envoy, once employed in Paris,
Bonner will soon be seen
As well known addict to the martyr's stake
For luckless heretics
In Mary's time: his mission was to break
The strong allegiance of her Protestant victims.

Now, he's inditing Wyatt for his role
Of traitor, who pursued the treacherous Pole.
(And suspect as a Protestant. How sound
In his conviction of the Real Presence?)
Wyatt is still amazed
At an attack having so little sense.
Never a traitor he
Now rising thirty-seven,
And long co-habiter with dear Bess Darell
By whom he has a son,
Living at Allington, a minor Heaven,
And suddenly swept into the ominous Tower
Must now prepare defence.

As was expected, Wyatt
Defends himself with confidence and brio
And a fine lack of whingeing,
Taking the war into the enemy's country
With, for these times, the minimum of cringing.

Reader — Subject as Bonner was to jealous rages
His old "mislikings" run to several pages.

Bonner — "I myslike it that
He is by evil company corrupted . . . "
"I myslike it that"
Heynes and myself by him were interrupted;
He greatly did discourage us by saying
"Ye shal doo no good with the Emperour . . . "

"And I myslike Mr Wiat
That out of England wrote
To Mr Mason—which by chance I sawe—
That he was made a Godde here by the Kinge
And by his Counsaill . . . "

"I myslike him
That he did go to see Grandevila first
Nor make us privy to what he did say . . .
(Though we were envoys with him all the way,
And I myself Lord Bishop)."

"And I myslike his calling to remembraunce"
Too often when in converse with the Emperour
"Emprisonment in the Towere,
Which seemeth so to stick within his stomacke
That he can not forget . . . "
(This argues more resentment than regret).

"I do myslike him that he did deceive us . . .
Grandvela saith 'What, more expostulation?'
'Yea, faith' quod Mr Wyat
'For unkinde handling of the Kynge in your trewce'.
Then he told us
That we should see the Emperour alone . . .
Yet hee next daye went to the Emperor's lodging
And from thence to Jonkaes
A place of nunnes, where solemn feast was kept,
And talking with the Emperour all the waye
After such merry sort and fasion",
Going along in such a joyefull manner
" 'Expostulation' turned into oblivion".

"A great marke that he shott at
To plese the Emperour and Grandevela,
And this he magnifyeth above all measure . . . "

Reader — Though Catholic, Bonner's a Puritan,
Complains of Wyatt—

Bonner — "Himself is given all upon pleasure . . .
Spending unthriftily on nunnes and harlots,
Keping the diets of his house too high . . . "

Bonner

And after failure over the Milan marriage
Wyatt was "herd to saye
By Goddes Bludde, ye shall see our master
Cast out at the cart's tail—
If so, he is well served"
And has so much deserved—
"He was so hott therein my stomacke boyled",
Bonner declared of Wyatt.
"Noo Sir, quoth I . . . "
And repremanded him for riding high.

Reader

In short, this jolly fellow, handsome Wyatt,
Gets on too well with Emperours and Kings
And is at home with continental courtiers,
Inclinded to laugh, and dance,
And generally to make merry with them.
If Wyatt indeed is bent,
If, after Aigues Mortes
He was thought traitor, why then was he sent
Ambassador to France?

So Bonner, in a self-deceived excitement
Had written once to Cromwell. And these things
Were now brought forward, making against Wyatt
Subsidiary inditement. But the whole,

Wyatt

The major charge was, that at Villa Franca
"I had collogued, once", with King Henry's cousin
The traitor Cardinal, Pole.

Reader

Arraigned for treachery in word and deed
By Bonner, who had been with him in Spain,

Wyatt

"Be not my judges and accusers bothe"
Wyatt besought the Council.

Reader

He'll explain
That all the traffic ever he had with Pole
Rebel and traitor—once, was to refuse
Some wine and gear he'd offered Wyatt as presents;
This was the whole.

Wyatt

And all these slanderers use a general rule
"Whom thou lovest not, accuse,
For though he heal the wound, the scars remain".

Friendship with Pole! No hint:
"Thou shalt as soon as find oil out of a flint
As find such thing in me . . . "
Shameless enough my words of "the cart's arse,
But I am wont to rap an oath or two",
And speak as most men do,
"I meant not any foul interpretation".

Wyatt	God knows what restless torment it has been Since hither coming, to examine myself Perusing all my deeds to my remembrance Whereby malicious enmity Might make an evil interpretation . . . When at Villa Franka I left no stone unturned to get intelligence Of what was doing at the court of Rome, Who were all there, working against my master And I feared for disaster . . . As touching Mr Mason— "I went with th'Emperour Upon the sea afore Marcels Commynge in a bote from Aquas Mortes In hasarde of the Mores and naughtie wether, By cause I would prevent Th'Emperor and the Frenche Kynge's meeting— But to breyke any thinge I cam to late." I never begged to be Ambassador, But for obedience to my sovereign master Would have refused it "Knowing that by my inability I should be wondrously encumbered, Being given To a more pleasant kind of life",
Reader	Here's Tom, unshriven From his old mocking and intemperate tongue; Too jolly, and unschooled In practised notions of diplomacy.
Wyatt	Come now, my lord of London Where's my abominable and vicious living? "I grant you I profess not chastity But yet I use not the abomination He charges me with nuns. Whoever heard of this, or who did see?" Lords of the Council, finally I ask you "Be not by any apprehension moved, The King's no tyrant, uses law with mercy". He never harmed lords who acquitted Dacres Though Dacres was a murderer well-proved.
Reader	So Wyatt set before them a long dish.
Wyatt	And to conclude—"fore God and all these men I charge you with my innocence and truth. As God defend, as ye If ye be guilty of mine innocent blood At his tribunal shall be inexcusable,

Wyatt

God put it in your hearts to judge of me
As I have willed towards the King my master
In heart and will and wish.''

Reader

Queen Catherine Howard pleaded now for Wyatt
Still sickened in the Tower; his excellence
Pleaded the louder. Soon he was released,
But Bonner's trumped-up charges not dismissed
Since Wyatt's told he must admit his guilt—
On this the frightened Council still insist.

Worse still, he must forever
Leave his beloved mistress,
Bess Darrell, and embrace his faithless wife,
Forgiving her adultery long since.
And this, on pain of death,
So rules his sovereign prince.

A curious order coming from King Henry
Always loath
For conjugal forgiveness, or embracing
A wife to whom he's long since given troth.
But Henry is a King, a man apart
And he alone may follow his wilful heart.

So Wyatt's wife returns
With pleasure or with tears?
Lord Cobham, who's her brother, long complained
That Wyatt's contribution to her upkeep
(Though hardly earned)
Has left too much to him.
And so these two, met after fifteen years.
Are left to sink or swim.

It can't have been all roses.
Maybe it was less tough than one supposes.

Small wonder Wyatt's lyric verses laud
The joys of self-containment, un-ambition,
''Quiet without let or stop
Unknown in court, that hath such brackish joys'',
Life in green places, on the grassy sward.

Perhaps his hard conditions were not forced:
The French Ambassador records his pardon

Castillon

''Pour estre personnage de bon esprit'',

Reader

Faithful in past, and useful for the future,
Which well could be.

Wyatt restored, made captain of three hundred
Of cavalry, to guard the town of Calais,

Reader

Acquiring property at Tintinhull
        Hoarding it for his boy,
Seems wholly to recover from his fall—
        But in his heart doth not.
Where is that native and abundant joy?

        The surface now is smooth;
        He's knight of the shire of Kent
        Member of Parliament,
        Captain of some eight vessels
        And then of twelve of the King's,
And ultimately admiral of all—
        His rise seems heaven-sent:

But Bess, perforce banished from Allington
        Comes no more to his call,
        Can be no more his joy,
Over all sexual spontaneity
        The sentence hangs its pall;
And he must turn, at peril of his head,
Back to that long-rejected marriage bed.

        Wyatt is free again;
But as he wrote, imprisoned in the Tower,
        "The scarrs remayne".

        Chastened, remote, he bears
A kind of un-healed sadness in the soul;
        And, between war's alarms,
He will translate the Penitential Psalms;
Never again laughing and confident
In the long ease of the heart,
In the untrammelled festival of love;
        Never again made whole.

Castillon

"A wonderful man", Castillon, new French envoy
Wrote home of Henry, to his king in France.
        "And having
Wonderful men about him . . . but he is
        An old fox."

Reader

And how thought Thomas Wyatt
So nearly wrecked on Henry's hidden rocks?
        Pacing his dangerous deck
And casting on his wife, newly restored
        To share his bed and board,
Whom he must love in peril of his neck,
        Hopeful or rueful glance?

Did he re-act with anger, lust, alarm?
Or did he shrug his shoulders, and exert
        The well-known charm
        On not the best of wives?

Reader

And never steal away again to Bess
And feel once more her warm encircling arm?
    Who knows? We only know
    Needs must when the devil drives.

29

Henry

Away once more to quell the restless North
I ride in splendour on a royal progress
    Through the late summer weather,
With harvests gathered, ploughmen going forth
In mists of morning, under sunshine tender,
    Autumn and hunting coming
    And summer all but past;
Through Hatfield, Lincoln, Boston, Hull, and York,
Where money and submissions came in fast.

A summer of St Luke, an Indian summer,
In weather, and the climate of the heart—
I went with martial music, archers, pikemen,
The Royal Guards in their Tudor splendour,
    And hunting as I passed;

Ill as I'd been, I made the great endeavour,
Happy with Catherine, cheerfully serene,
    And working all the time
As if that youthful love could last forever.

Alas! My wife was hunting other game,
A deer called Dereham, she'd made secretary,
    Culpeper, her young kinsman,
Young bloods, ready for dares,
For music, for love-meetings on the stairs;
    She's writing fatal love-notes
    In her still childish hand,
Folly that no stern judge would understand.
And soon her guilt is proved by iron men
Who know no pity; and I myself who loved her
    Deaf to her cries and prayers.

Reader

Norfolk's long face is several inches longer
His niece is now abandoned to her fate;
    His stepmother,

Dowager, Duchess of Norfolk

The Duchess in the Tower, is somewhat stronger,
And furiously indignant at the cold,
    Complains about her room
And that her family is being overcrowded:
    And, although much to blame
For the poor Queen's predicament and shame,
Does nothing but these grievances relate.

Reader — Its ***sauve qui peut*** amongst the House of Howard.

*   *   *   *

Reader — Cranmer was sent to break the news to Catherine
And, moved by her wild tears
Tells her to plead her pre-contract with Dereham
Before her marriage, and thus ease her fears
And save her life;
For this would only mean
A close confinement in a nunnery,
If she had never in law been the King's wife.
Catherine would none of this;
Hoping perhaps to see the King, and plead,
Winning him with her kiss;
Or possibly too proud to face suggestion
That she was never Queen.

But men more cruel
Day after day crammed Henry's ears with detail
Of everything most bad,
As gloating on the scurrilous reports
Of his young wife and her accomplished lovers,
As if their only purpose
Had been to drive him mad.

"Lilies that fester . . . " (those words yet un-written)
"Smell far worse than weeds".

Henry — Nothing so sour as that which once was sweet;
Deeply aggrieved those who were deeply smitten,
And duly fierce their deeds.

Blind in their rage, men will forget the goodness
Brooding upon the wrong;
Blind as a bat to others' bitter grief.

Men suffer; but how many suffer long?

*   *   *   *

Henry — All Soul's Day, and in Hampton Court's fine chapel
I'd thanked God for the happy life I led
With Catherine, "the Rose without a Thorn",
As I was fond of saying;
Gentle, she seemed, and innocent, and sweet
And fresh as flowers are when girls go maying,
With her I hoped my life would be complete.

The greater was the disillusionment.
Dreadful the end of dreaming.
She sang so sweetly under the summer trees
But sung for other men. Our time was short.

Henry

And yet I loved her
After a fashion . . . still can hear her screaming
Down the long galleries of Hampton Court.

At first the news of Catherine and her sin
I met at first with scornful disbelief . . .
Slowly the truth grew plainer,
Came homing uncontrollably within.
This pit wherein I'm hurled
These stakes on which I lie
Usual enough, but they are no less sharp.
Black jealousy
Is the enormous devil of the world.

What balm can ease pride of its dark contusion?
Terrible anger, the twin face of love
Rises like Janus in my scalded heart
And looks both ways in furious confusion.

Revenge the one, the permanent solution.

Sometimes I am a cauldron of hot rage . . .
And long for torments, fierce as I inflict
On heresy's lost sheep,
To fall on my false wife . . .
Again, I weep,
Refuse delights, shun the escape of sleep.

My fellows were enormously embarrassed
To see me weep in Council, send for a sword
To slay this dearly loved. I ordered horses
Not knowing where to bid them carry me,
Removed far distant from my normal courses
Of food, and love, hunting and policy.

I talked of torture; and then wept anew
As one beside himself.
Why was she such a fool as marry me
Putting herself in pawn to so much gossip
Too many knowing minds?
I am beyond myself with disappointment
My glory outraged, and my hope destroyed—
Woe to the strumpet whom ambition blinds!

Nothing to satisfy me but revenge.
Ahead, a loveless void.

Others had plucked this blossom of the Howards
Too long entrusted to the foul old Duchess
Or ever she came to me: and others found
Old promises fulfilled,
Caring no whit for me
Daring to love and daring to be killed.

Reader

Mannock and Dereham, musical Culpeper
Are tried and tortured, and will soon confess,
Are then dispatched, and upon London Bridge
Their severed heads are spiked.
Catherine as well confessing
And passing slowly down the tidal river
Towards the Tower, can see the grim remains
Of these brave fellows whom she too much liked.

Henry

I was too shaken to see anyone.
I kept myself apart to brood and mope,
Often to weep . . . And yet immune to mercy
For that young foolish girl
That thornless flower
Weeping unheard within the icy Tower
For the brief dangerous glory that had been.

Unyielding, as men sentenced her to sleep
Beyond love's waking and love's recompense,
Love's quickening, love's renewing,
Beyond the laughter and the stir of sense
And all that joy that had been her undoing,
Wanton and lax.

Her sentence I confirmed.
So dies she . . . and my youth, and ageing hopes
Fell with the falling axe.

In death, they rumour, she forgot herself,
Her youth, her peril, her extremity;
Begged only for her kinsmen in their danger
To the King's love now stranger.
She made provision for her faithful servants,
Spoke no harsh words of me.

Here was a generous love

Reader

To which somehow, he never found the key.

What is he weeping for? One pretty girl?
Or his own powers' decay?
The failure of the gallant barque of hope?
For vanishing virility at bay?

Henry

A silly wanton, asking for her fate,
A plump sweet partridge, with her downy feathers,
All hazel eyes, and folly.
Don't speak of her, it makes me melancholy.

But was I grieving more for failing manhood
For lost and lusty youth,
Than for the fate of this slain childish girl?
Who now can know the truth?

Henry

Briefly I grieved for Catherine, it seems,
Or for myself, and for love's dreaded failing,
And for the bitter wakening from its dreams . . .

Sometimes, again, I hear that frightened wailing.

* * * *

Henry

Regret and pity won a fleeting glance.
        A very few days after
        I felt the need for laughter,
And summoned twenty-six of the best court ladies
        To banqueting and dance.

        And that is how it goes.
Life must go ***on***, for all domestic woes.

The mainland monarchs scarce could hide their mocking,
Rogue tongue in roguish cheeks, they did not blame,
Wishing me better luck another time.

Francis

''Lightness of women'', wrote the King of France
''Cannot impugn the honour of us men''.

Henry

And very soon I was myself again.

The world is wide, and ripe for enterprise
That's unconcerned with women, old or new.
I sent for Chapuys, gave him a review
Masterly in its grasp and thoroughness
Of Europe's state, from Buda to Dunkirk.
        He was amazed
At this astonishing recuperation
As I continued, nation after nation.

        I told him plainly
How Emperor Charles, his great and gouty master
        Had bungled at Algiers
Through ignorant pilots—a pretty piece of work
That might reduce his admirals to tears;
Even stout Cortez' plans were disregarded.

And how King Francis, double-faced as ever,
        Leading the tawdry French
        Was treating with the Turk,
        A most unChristian thing
        For the most Christian King
His duty towards Christendom to burk!
The while the Crescent sweeps through Eastern Europe
        And for a new crusade
        The frightened church bells ring.
        The Turks have taken Buda
        And are assaulting Pest,

Henry — And where this conquest ends
The Lord alone knows best.

Reader — Is this still Christendom, or something other?
France, whose brave Charles Martel
Once halted them at Tours
And saved us from the hell
Of conquest by the Moors,
That France should league against a Christian brother
Fighting in desperation for his life!

Dark faces under turbans, scimitars
Under green banners tossed,
The shouting tumult of that fierce advance—
Vienna threatened, Pest and Buda lost,
The Crescent moon arising, the Cross tumbling;
On smouldering plains, the scattered homesteads burned.
The Pope abetted once,
So now does France;
How is this tide of Islam to be turned?

Henry — Certainly not by me.
Time now to run the spotlight on the sea
Because the clever Francis
Is cooking another goose,
He's founded the great harbour of Le Havre,
"Seeking the Trade of spicery by a shorter way
Than any that the Portingales do use",
Makes for the northern ice and the St Lawrence—
Here's a sea mastery I now might lose . . .
And his betrayal of Charles
In favour of the Turks,
Is but a part of his colonial ruse.
The continent has lost my interest.

More daring and more distant fields unfold;
And then, politely, I informed Chapuys
That I am now sufficient to myself,
Owing his Emperor neither help nor gold.
Often in other days
I looked to Charles for help, discovered none.
These mighty leagues of Europe leave me cold.

There's still a league against me, I am told;
To me, that is all one.
***Va bene, Je M'en fiche*.**
Neither the Swede nor Dane,
Linked though they be with France, can do me harm.
And Frederick, the Dane, "at least, is old"
The ocean is the field to stretch my arm.
With my great ships
I shall, in time, effect the French eclipse.

30

Reader

Stronger than brandy, or than flowing wine,
    Power intoxicates;
Turning men mad, and greedier than swine.

Power over children, or subordinates.
Power over wife, or husband, or the old,
Sweetest of all, power over erstwhile mates.

The priestly power of faith over the people,
The power to terrify the luckless folk
Who rock the roots of our particular steeple.

The sense of righteousness that dominates.
The power of riches, used in scorn or folly,
The power that plays with other people's fates,

Power over radicals who cause disruption—
Who can resist the cancer growth of power
It subtle, slow, invisible corruption?

Henry

And above all, I have to exercise it
    On those who once I loved
    And lavished kindness on,
    Thinking that they loved ***me***—
    The more deceived to be.
Sir Thomas More, my cousin Reginald Pole,
And Henry Norris, and Sir Thomas Wyatt,
    And those two sad young Howards—
The thornless Catherine, much loved Anne Boleyn—
And there were others precious to my soul
    None of them fools or cowards
Who roused the furious devil that sleeps within.

Planning my movements always most astutely
I rode a highway without pause or pity,

Reader

A process leading surely and minutely
To absolute power corrupting absolutely.
So that when some unfortunate's arrested
He sends his men to seize on all their goods
Even before a trial has found them guilty.
    No mercy for old loyalty.
    No feeling for old loves;
    His heart is now immovably congested.

* * * *

Henry

    Now for United Kingdom
"Robberies, murders, thefts and malefacts"
In Wales I have suppressed; and sent J.P.s
With English law instead of tribal custom.

Henry — The Welsh may rise against it—we shall see.
Since I'm half Welsh, they take a lot from me.

Reader — The phantom of the past, with its long fingers
Seizing the willing heart,
Within the Irish mind still closely lingers
Refusing to let go.

Henry — Why ever did the Pope
Encourage my great forbear to the full
—Henry Plantagenet—to arm and send
His Norman knights, and follow them himself
To an ill-fated Ireland,
To turn the wild confusion into order?
"Subdue and rule" comands the Papal Bull—
And so began a problem without end.

When I was young and certain I knew best
I'd told my Lord Lietutenant to be kind,
Not wanting enemies to north ***and*** west.

"Politic ways, and aimiable persuasions
Founded on law and reason"
I urged on him; thinking that "rigorous dealings"
Can but arouse men's pride and angry feelings.

Bent on the unity of all the Isles
I wooed the wildness of the land with smiles.

The Lord-Lieutenant, certain he knew better,
Answered my letter—

Mountjoy — "Only by conquest can this land be brought
Into good order, into due subjection,
Give me the men, and I will solve the matter."

Henry — Arming for France—though this I didn't mention—
I lacked the men, as well as the intention.

Better, meanwhile, just to accept what's there
Of government and law, however scant
And out of tune with the rest of Western Europe,
And quite haphazard in its intervention
Between the victim and the murderer.

The rule of Garret Oge, the great FitzGerald
May not be strictly fair,
So murmurs my adviser;
But just for now, its wiser
To leave the rule of the land to King Kildare.

In riper years I see what Mountjoy meant.
For 'Silken Thomas', in his gaudy gear,

Henry

Untruly told by Ormonde that his father
Had been by me destroyed within the Tower,
        Has brought the rebels out,
Plumped for the Pope, and then, besieging Dublin
        Has butchered my Archbishop on the strand.

Massacre followed, at my army's hand,
And the wild Geraldines are put to rout.

Reader

Conveyed to England, hoping to make terms,
Betrayed by his safe conduct, all were killed—
The nephew Thomas and his five young uncles
Swung from a silken rope above the Thames—
        But for what reason?

Henry

Arn't they all guilty of the cost of treason?
The blood of holy men, as they should know
        Is never to be spilled
        (Unless, that is, I spill it).

Reader

All the Kildares are gone (Save one small boy
Safely conveyed to Italy through France
And growing up less Irish than the rest).

Henry

        So here's the chance
        We must be up and doing
        Before more trouble's brewing;
This is no moment to avert the glance.

For God's sake, let the Irish bards stop singing
Night after night, of ancient pride and wrongs.
Where is the future leading, for wild hearts
        Nursed on such songs?

Subdue, and then deal gently with the Irish,
        Proclaim myself their king—
        Such was my hope;

Reader

Which foundered, as so many were to do
On their long loyalty towards the Pope.

Henry

Just as Gustavus Vasa has in Sweden
I will dissolve the Irish monasteries
And spend the money on good government
Whether the Irish want it or they don't.

Whether there's anger in the hut or hall
I'll force my settlement upon them all—
        And then start wooing.

I take the lords of Ireland by the hands;
These are no kerns; "pregnant and subtle wits"

Henry

I called the chieftains, and where such men lead
Men gradually follow.
Re-granting them their titles and their lands
Brings Desmond and O'Neill to our opinion,
And Ormonde and McWilliam follow suit;
Such planning isn't hollow.
For Ireland left alone
Will fall an easy prey to Spain or France
(Or, in due course, to Germany or Russia).
Forming a bridgehead, from which to advance
And do us all a mischief.
Here is my firm opinion
United we will stand, divided fall—
I'll make this wayward country my dominion.

"Infinite treasure I exhausted here"
Reforming Ireland, I was soon to write.
And it was wasted time,
And wealth ill-spent.
For through King James of Scotland, my young nephew,
My sister Margaret's son
The troubles were begun.

Two Spanish Jesuits James allowed to land
And pass through Scotland,
Upon conversion bent,
Salmeron and Casata;
Each grimly ready to become a martyr,
Their powerful persuasions will not cease.
And here's no middle class to be enriched
By Abbey lands, and so become involved
In seeing that my settlement's not ditched.
So there's an end of peace.

Reader

How is it that we people of the West
Cannot believe that someone else knows best?

That dogged independence, and the ghost
Of long past glories haunt us like sweet music
The half-forgotten tune we love the most?

Henry

No matter: soon my ships will found afar
One or another English-speaking nation,
Shelter for Scots, Welsh, Irish emigration.
And here, to admiration,
They'll stretch their legs, and stretch their lively minds
(Only, alas, they'll nurse their indignation).

Just for the time I sorted out the Irish
And tidied old confusion—never doubt it—
Causing undying wrath
For the imperious way I set about it.

Henry

Nothing in this green country can endure
Except their faith, their music, and their charm,
And an unchanging taste for doing harm
        Entirely for harm's sake.
        For they themselves are born
And live and die in ceaseless disputation.
Strife is the hobby of this lively nation.

So be it; and at least I kept them quiet
        While I brought forth
My long unfolding purpose further north.

United Kingdom—England, Ireland, Wales
        And Scotland presently,
Securely organized, my strong son ruling,
        Good churches, and good schooling,
        And reasonable laws—
Towards such anchorage I trim my sails.
A thing so beneficial to them all
        Will surely come to be.

Though overlaid by fat ferocity
Becoming fairly terrible to see,
My purpose held—the rule of proper laws.
This stayed my ruling, fixed, philosophy,
And men have lived for many a meaner cause.

31

Henry

        Difficulties increased,
Under the slow, stern, ache of middle age—
Lonely, suspicious, prone to jealousy
        And sudden furious rage.
Always well-cushioned, always overfed,
But never under-exercised, or lax,
        And not diseased,
        Heavily gross, and gouty,
        I was still doughty:
Though in my leg an ulcer had developed
        Whose pain but rarely eased.

And those who know not pain and its temptations
To dark suspicions and sharp irritations
Are no fit judges upon those who do;
To whom each morning dawns without fresh gladness
        Only with pains anew.

        Courts are not kindergartens.
Here, where so often laughing mouth belies
The icy circumspection of the eyes,

Henry

How many plot and plan?
Wherever power dwells
How many are the baby Machiavels?

Goodness and truth are fine, if you can share them
With kindly company.
Long is the tale of regicide disasters.
Truth in the inner soul is wonderful,
So also mercy. But how great a number
Of these proud men in plumed magnificence,
Renaissance beaux, who love the smell of power,
Walking with care the halls of princely masters
Waiting the timely hour,
Do truly wear them?

Judge not, cold men in heated libraries,
In learned, cramped, self-righteous cogitations
How deep the fathoms of my wickedness.
You have not had, can never hope to have
One tenth of my temptations!

One thing, sweet gentlemen, is crystal clear—
Kings who can't rule by love must rule by fear:
And since the Pope no longer loves my name
I'm anybody's game.

Try sticking closely to Christ's admonitions
When sorting out a ragbag of petitions!
It cannot well be done;
However much you feel the Holy Spirit
Or worship still the Father and the Son.

Try as we will, the ruler is but man,
Doing imperfectly the best he can.

Reckless to folly in the joust or hunt
At other times I walked the world with care
Over-suspicious of the predators,
Little inclined to spare
Men who but faltered with a careless word,
Or did a thoughtless action.
And so, with power for nearly forty years
I am still there.

My majesty held fast
To the grim last.

* * * *

Henry

Since Flodden, I'd conciliated Scots,
Hoping their ardour would be thus abated.
And though my sister, widowed there, is dead,
I've wooed her son, being so near related.

Henry

But James has steadily refused to see me,
And married two French wives, and played along
With every Frankish ploy,
Even refused to meet me
Without a permit sealed by the French King;
In short, has done his utmost to annoy.

No-one's suggesting that the boy should greet me
Extravagantly warm in his affections;
But he's my nephew, now more man than boy.
I am no spider and he is no fly:
Kings above all should hold to royal connections.

And now the Pope, who hates me quite as strongly
As I hate him, remits the Scottish dues
To Rome, for full two years,
So that young Jamie forthwith has the cash
To loose attack upon me, whom Paul names
"Son of perdition, and of Satan son
Who now bears himself
As King of England . . . "
This allows King James
To win immense ***reclame***
Cutting a splendid anti-English dash.

Reader

Money's to hand, oxen for gun-carriages,
Both Highlanders and Lowlanders are led
Eagerly southward to high-walled Carlisle
Under the fullness of a hunter's moon.

But English cavalry attacks too soon . . .

There had been raid, and again counter-raid
Some while, along the Border,
With very little of success or order,
Before this second Flodden, at Solway Moss.

Henry

And Pope Paul doesn't know
That luckless James is now already dead,
Killed not by me but by the wound of failure.

Reader

Thirty years old, and sped by no disease
The Scots King dies at Falkland, of despair,
Leaving a baby, Mary, Queen of Scots,
As his unlucky heir.
And not the longed-for son.

Henry

So be it. She can marry my boy Edward
And bring the warring kingdoms into one.

Dealing discreetly with the Scottish lords
Who still survive, I entertain them grandly

Henry

In London, since I hope to keep them still,
Whilst I pursue my endless war with France.
"I show you kindness for unkindness, here,
And right for wrong . . ." I blandly told the Scots.
"It would beseem my kingly honour ill
To war upon the dead, or on a widow
Or a poor suckling fallen on mischance."

None of which curbed me in the proclamation
That I was King of this unruly nation.

They rose against me; I could scarce believe it.
          And crowned their baby Queen
As if the Solway fight had never been,
And soon they sent the little girl to France
Out of my range, to marry with the Dauphin:
Rejecting my son Edward for their King—
          A most presumptuous thing.

Well, I have other wars; and they must learn;

Reader

So Edinburgh, their fortress town, will burn,
Jedburgh and Holyrood in flames as well;
The Lowlands will be ravaged in their turn.

Henry

Painful no doubt, but their French dowager
Mary of Guise, has acted with false guile
          Sending away the Queen, the baby Mary.
Why at the start, did they attack Carlisle?

* * * *

Henry

Some men learn very slowly. I was one.
          So, a last fling for France,
Even although we raise the price of gold.
Long since, I have dispersed the wealth untold
The monasteries yielded, and the sum
Enormous, that my careful father left.
Although it cost the value of my throne
          I still must have Boulogne.
Calais, essential bridgehead, cannot stand
Unless Boulogne should likewise come to hand.

Fair stood the wind. Last in a long long line
Of English Kings holding the same design
          To claim their own
          Of the fair land of France,

I left from Portsmouth, handsomely regaled;
          Gentry, nobility, and yeomanry
          In force were shown,
And fifty experts from a Cornish tin-mine
          To undermine Boulogne.

Henry

War never daunted my belief in learning,
And so before I sailed
I added to the happiness of nations
By two superb foundations.

Wolsey's old work completing, I now launched
Christ Church at Oxford, with its flowery meadow,
Trinity College, Cambridge, still both wearing
My stalwart image in their place of honour,
And my proud arms still bearing.

Reader

The rain in France fell mainly near Boulogne
That long July. Small comfort from the Dutch.
Expensive cavalry from Germany
Behaved too badly and devoured too much.

Chapuys

"Nevertheless" Chapuys reported drily
"The King has better health and he works better,
More than I would have thought".

Henry

Slipping and stumbling in continous mud,
Riding to Marquise in a thunderstorm
Further than Cap Gris Nez,
We battered on against the stubborn fort.

Boulogne fell in September. The surrender
Taken by me; the Master of the Horse
Standing before me with a naked sword.
Though promised safety, many refugees
Trudged out before me on their weary course.
Storm after storm contributed more mud,
Felled the pavilions, levelled many trees.
Yet marching in with Spanish Albuquerque
I felt a surge of triumph and heart's ease—

Calais safeguarded surely, and Boulogne
Garrisoned by my men;
Along the Pas de Calais my writ ran.

Nothing in war is static for five minutes.
The rain continued, and the rows began.

The Emperor, most slily,
Made a great treaty, right behind my back
And left me to the mercy of the French,
Hugely outnumbered, deeply vulnerable.
They naturally, next summer,
With fleet and army launched a great attack.

Gathering to himself the might of Spain
And speaking from a comfortable distance,

Emperor Charles

"We have done nothing" wrote the Emperor
"Of which the King of England can complain".

Henry

My men were furious but still defiant.
"It shall not enter yet into my creed
That Frenchmen cope with us" one noble wrote.
Its true enough, our ships are still afloat.
But these fine words were buoyed by little deed.
        "I asked Chapuys",
Telling me of his master's real good faith
As I was making ready to embark,
Why did the fellow keep me in the dark?

Sickness at Calais, ships that need careening,
"Frays with the Almaynes", and continued rains
Is all the news from France, this dark November.
Nil desperandum; we must stick it out.
With many details, and fresh complications
Of bulwarks and of flanks about Boulogne
        I told them how to better
The ramparts, and make good the fortifications,
To thwart these pesky continental nations.

        But come December
I celebrated Christmas-tide at Greenwich
In the strange bliss a happy marriage brings,
        At peace with all my children
        Cheerful as we could be
By the great river rolling to the sea,
        Dark under winter stars.
As merry a Christmas as I can remember.

32

Henry

Queen Catherine Parr—she is my comfort now,
        The wife whom none confronted
Save Anne of Cleves, who felt herself affronted.
This widow as "not near so beautiful"
As she herself, and without hope of children,
Having borne none to both her previous husbands,
Anne grumbled. "A fine burden
Madam has taken on herself" she scolded,
Coarsely alluding to my growing weight.
        But she complains too late.

Pleased with myself, I'd taken a wedded wife
"With none opposing and with all applauding"
The widowed Catherine Parr, at Hampton Court
This last July, new happiness affording
        To my long last of life.

Hope is the solace of the sanguine mind.
This time at last, my hope is surely founded;
Passion or pride no longer leave me blind.

Henry

So to the Bishop of that long cathedral
Time-honoured Winchester,
Whose chancel holds the bones of many Kings,
On this most fortunate day,
Hopeful forever, with ***"Hilari vultu"***
"A joyful countenance" I answered, "Yea".

Perilous still, as are the slums at night
Of some strange city,
My ever-brilliant court
Alive with music, poetry, discourse,
Wide and high learning, is now set alight
By her, my truly educated Queen,
Making these things, as I do, her delight;
As well as dealing kindly with my children.

And they, and doubtless many courtiers too
Thanked all the saints there are
For clever and persuasive Catherine Parr.

* * * *

Henry

My land, next summer, was again alarmed.
Through all my life, peril has been no stranger
But here's the ultimate, astringent danger.
A hundred ships are gathered at Le Havre
And fifty floats, artillery and hackbutts,
Thousands of gallant Frenchmen, fully armed
For our invasion.

And not this alone,
Continually they threaten at Boulogne;
Meanwhile the Scots, alive to French persuasion
While that malignant Guise is in control—
Start to attack again;
Defeat us at Dumbarton and at Jedburgh,
On Ancram Moor a thousand men are slain.

(Admittedly, we'd captured twenty vessels
Afloat with Bordeaux wine
And brought them into London with the spoils
Last autumn, which may possibly account
For warlike French design.)

* * * *

Henry

A calm July, faint haze along the Channel,
And off the Isle of Wight
Hundreds of sails of Frenchmen, heavy armed,
Here to take Portsmouth as their landing site.

What can our bowmen do, however brave
Against their musquets, and their armoury?

Henry

Will the wind rise, and save?

I was at dinner in my ship ***Great Harry***,
Quickly I went ashore
The better to control the strategy
As all made ready to attack at sea.

And still, the sultry forenoon thwarted us,
The breathless day wore on . . .

Moveless the ***Harry*** lay, and ***Mary Rose*** . . .
Shared the repose.

Only the subtle movements of the tide
Whispered along ***Great Harry's*** curving side.

Only the galliasses, "rowing pieces",
Could come at them, and they'd be lost alone.

Never a breath of wind. The heat increases . . .

The ports of all the ships
Lay open, to attract the slightest breeze
And cleanse them with the sweetness of the seas.

Four of the afternoon . . . the day near gone.

When suddenly, a hopeful puff of wind
Comes from the West, and soon its power increases.
Like an enormous swan
Great Harry now is moving.

But horror beyond thought—
A deadly, unbelievable surprise!
The ***Mary Rose***, listing with heavy guns
And just now going about,
Is flooded through each open lower port
And sinks before my eyes.

If ever I knew despair it was now
As slowly but remorselessly she goes . . .
Pride of my heart, the glorious ***Mary Rose***.
Watching the disappearance of her prow
I cried aloud in anguish at the sight!

Reader

But no cries can her weight of water lighten
Or slack ropes tighten.

Henry

Sir George Carew and full four hundred men
With this great ship went under.
Thirty or less survived.
And, turning from despair
My huge wrath broke like thunder.

Henry

Deliverance!
For now the west wind rising
Scared the French Admiral, who drove up Channel.
Those many forts and stakes of my devising
Had made the coast secure;
And after burning Brighton, he's obliged
To turn aside off Dover
And sail once more for Havre—
Immediate peril's over.

Even the Scots are quiet;
Who in a furious riot
(Handsomely helped by me),
Have murdered their pugnacious Cardinal
St Andrews' David Beaton,
And hung his salted body from a wall
For all to see.

Yet after all the efforts, lives and gold,
Soon after I was dead, Boulogne was sold
And of necessity
Calais and Guisnes would follow very soon.
And so concluded that eternal dream
Of lands in France, of monarchy, of rule,
Of crying for the moon.

* * * *

Henry

Age offers no deliverance from the sins
To which our youth afforded anchorage.

Those who were cruel are more vindictive now;
All that impatient anger that I harbour
Grows wilder, in a fierce attempt to cow
Our luckless entourage.
Our Council and our Ministers, our barber,
Our surgeon, horse-boy, groom;
Lenience has no room
We seek by fear
To win that care which love will not endow.

Love did I say? I had forgotten Catherine . . .
Perhaps she never loved me; but, if not
She was love's kind and calm impersonation,
As if my past misdeeds were all forgot.

I suffered much from women, old and young
And they from me; but she, with lack of fear
And lack of forwardness or discontent
Became love's instrument,
Came between me and my worst indignation.

Henry

Even a bandage and a bowl of gruel
From gentle hands, and a soft persuasive tongue
Can make the grip of helplessness less cruel.
And soothe the heart, and keep the pain at bay.
Others might bend to my untramelled will
    —Issuing edicts over life and death
    With my last breath—
    Catherine was calm and still,
    She braved the reign of terror;
Living devotedly from day to day
Seemingly unconcerned with making hay.

Reader

In her compassion he was greatly blessed,
    God grant to all such blessing—
A kindness undistressed and undistressing,
As the mist thickens over earthly hopes
And wild ambition, as the warm sun slopes
Deliberate and unhalting to the west.

33

Reader

A warm October, fifteen forty-two.
De Courrières, a Spanish envoy, landing
Unusually, and punctually, at Falmouth
    Takes the King by surprise.
Wyatt, who is well looked upon in Spain,
Is sent to meet him. Riding hard, with relays
Of horses posted for him, in endeavour
    Not to arrive too late,
Sweats heavily, is chilled, and takes a fever
    And in three days, he dies,
At Sherborne, in strong illness
    Aged barely thirty-eight.

Few were the friends who were not deeply saddened,
    A stream of verse pours forth.
Its as if only rhyming couplets, sonnets,
   Can truly tell his worth.

Lord Surrey

"Wyatt resteth here that quick[1] could never rest,
Whose heavenly gifts increased by disdain,
And virtue sank the deeper in his breast,
Such profit he of envy could obtain.

A head where wisdom mysteries did frame
Whose hammers beat still in that lively brain
As on a stithy,[2] where some work of fame
Was daily wrought, to turn to Britain's gain.

1 alive
2 forge

Lord Surrey

A visage stern and mild where both did grow
Vice to condemn, in virtues to rejoice;
Amid great storms, whom grace assured so
To live upright, and smile at fortune's choice.

A hand that taught what might be said in rhyme
That reft Chaucer the glory of his wit,
A mark the which (unperfected for time)
Some may approach but never none shall hit.

A tongue that served in foreign realms his king,
Whose courteous talk to virtue did enflame
Each noble heart, a worthy guide to bring
Our English youth by travail into fame.

An eye whose judgment no effect could blind
Friends to allure, and foes to reconcile,
Whose piercing look did represent a mind
With virtue fraught, reposed, void of guile.

A heart where dread yet never so oppressed
To hide the thought that might the truth advance,
In neither fortune lost, nor so repressed
To swell at wealth, nor yield unto mischance.

A valiant corps where force and beauty met,
Happy, alas, too happy but for foes,
He lived and ran the race that nature set
Of manhood's shape, where she the mould did lose.

But to the heavens that simple soul is fled
Which left with such as covet Christ to know.
Witness of faith that never shall be dead,
Sent for our wealth, but not received so.
    Thus for our guilt this jewel we have lost,
    The earth his bones, the heavens possess his ghost."

Reader

    So wrote the poet Surrey
Surrey the Catholic, and far the younger;
Wyatt, aspiring Protestant, who yet
    Were able to be friends
    In this dire age of burnings;
    Were able to forget
The rack, the torments, all those terrible ends
    Of bloody and unnecessary death.

Their poetry, their courage, and their honour
Twinned them beyond the ravages of faith.

    And many voices, as a fall of petals
    Over green honoured graves
        Serenely lies,
    Echo his praises, until echo dies—

1st Poet
"Wyatt the wise, the learned and the good"

2nd Poet
"Wyatt to starry regions did ascend
Ere forty years acomplished had their end."

John Leland
"Wyatt the nonpareil,
Who Britain's glory showed
From whose melodious mouth
The well-tuned verses flowed . . . "

4th Poet
"Holbein, the chiefest of that curious Art,
Drew Wyatt's lively image in each part
With matchless skill; but not Appelles can
Portray the wit and spirit of the man."

John Leland
" . . . Shall grim death
Sever our minds? O let it not be so.
Farewell, beloved Wyatt, a long farewell . . . "

Reader
Over his grave the petals float and linger
Falling serene and soft—

5th Poet
"Wyatt, the matchless knight",

John Leland
"Our bravest youth,
He is the flower of wit, and he is ours",

6th Poet
" . . . now lament
With a just sorrow, that Wyatt, who was for us
The light of good counsel, has been snatched away."

John Leland
"Wyatt, that rare bird"
"Our Wyatt bears the palm of eloquence."
"O Wyatt thou has conquered warrior's spears",
"How can we say that Wyatt's not alive
When monuments of his genious still survive?"

"Wyatt was like the bird of Jupiter
Who seeks the highest and most difficult."

"The court gave spotless Wyatt many friends,
But three, above all, he chose out himself:
He honoured Poynings for his generous heart,
He took delight in Blage's subtle mind,
He valued Mason for his radiant learning.
And these now mourn the dead with floods of tears,
Crying 'Dear Wyatt' with a threefold voice."

7th Poet
"Wyatt, the topmost crown of virtue"

8th Poet
"The often jesting, never jeering Tom."

John Leland
"Wyatt the source, the lightning and the light
Of eloquence . . . "

9th Poet
"Noble Wyatt,
The darling of the earth, has died to-day."

John Leland

"The Emperor Charles is wont to praise
His matchless powers and eloquence,
His manners simple and sincere,
His genius and his perfect sense
Of honour: others share this view
And hold his estimate as true."

"Nature made Wyatt tall, with powerful muscles
And sinews strong; adding thereto a face
As beautiful as any. On his brow
Serene, played joyful lights, like starbeams bright.
His mass of hair was golden in his youth,
But afterwards he lost it by degrees . . . "

"Wyatt in noble things
Was worthy of his country while he lived
And is her ornament now he is Dead."

Reader

Doubtless his praise lost nothing in the telling;
Even allowing this,
His requiem, widely swelling,
Compounds a very loving farewell kiss.

* * * *

Henry

Hearing of Wyatt's death
Old envy falters briefly in my breast,
Sorrow awhile takes hold;
When shall we see again
Such wit and wisdom, liveliness and zest,
Such readiness to jest?

Surrey

"Wyatt resteth here, that quick could never rest."

Wyatt

"My call and cry to you is honesty,
Honesty,
Wisdom, and gentleness, and friendliness,
Desire for good,
And, above all, the truth."

Reader

Some men are like ambassadors
From a far country of the past or future
A land of faith and troth;
Half understanding, half interpreting,
But deep in love with both.

Before the ripeness of accomplishment
Far hence is Wyatt gone, from far was sent;
Far from the music that he might have made,
His bright flame early spent
His fame made brief and hollow.

And his poet friend
The charming wilful Surrey soon will follow.

PART SEVEN

34

Henry

Stony as diamonds, or as adamant,
Rock hard, and ever harder I am grown,
Supremacy become my core and being,
Drawing the state unto myself alone.

(Well, you're acquainted with the other thing
Henry the Sixth, the weak and saintly King,
When universal misery was known.)

I am supreme; and my supremacy
In Church, as little to be called in question
As my unchallenged right upon the throne.

And who denies either supremacy
        Is equally the traitor
        Is equally suborned.
        Friends, adversaries, prelates,
Children and subjects, you have all been warned.

Defender of the Faith, I still insisted;
Attacker had become the Pope of Rome.
Worship was part of life, and I yet loved
The pageant of religion, found release
In every form of ritual that existed,
In all prostrations, dramas of repentance,
The dance and ceremony of our faith,
Confessing a selection from my sins
Still certain where one ends and one begins.

In all of this I struggled to appease
A jealous God waiting for fragile prey—
Twice daily begged his mercy on my knees.

        Listen, before I sink
To dread and possible senility.
Kings are not gods. They feel more furious anger
Being men, with blood and fever in their veins,
When they are cheated in the marriage bed
        Than common man might think.

Disgrace is public, open to all disdains.
And it was long before my love of pleasures
Turned to delight in other people's pains.

I followed a set purpose in my land;
One Pope might quarrel, and the next forgive;
        And reconciliation
Was always on the cards, you understand,
If they would take me at my own valuation.

Henry

It was most needful to leave lawful children
To hold the country from a civil war
More lethal than the one that went before
Because the Church would also take a hand.

And yet my faith had always been my pride!
All my long life I lived a Catholic,
So to the end professed, and so I died.
What if ***one*** Pope should override?

Popes are not Medes and Persians
What one affirms another may deny;
The faith once given runs to several versions.

Leo the Tenth promised to sanctify
My father as the rightful King of France,
But ends by giving a French King Milan.
Much is expediency and sophistry—
    Catch as catch can!

Clement the Seventh faced with a decision
Could operate as well as any juggler
    Keeping three balls in the air;
    What holiness is there?
Where is Saint Peter? Where the heavenly vision?

I knew what moved the general English heart
    And took its part;
Not always in the manner recommended
By men who operate below a steeple.
For forty years but two, through strain and stress,
I ruled this difficult country, this tough people,
Without an army and without police.
My methods were peculiar, none the less
I ruled through Parliament and by consent
(Even although, at times, it would be bent).

I ruled by magnetism and address
    I held my folk in thrall
The cleverest and strongest of them all,
And, give or take a row or two, in peace—
My force of personality, my charm
Covered the country like a golden fleece.

And still, and still, for all my executions,
Spending of riches, poured away like water,
    Unkindness to my daughter,
My cruel halt to the Pilgrimage of Grace,
Men yet ran hotly to behold my face,
Men cheered me everywhere when I rode forth
Wearing the aureole of majesty;

Henry

As if this triumph of magnificence
Touched a dim sense
In that huge shouting heart
Of being themselves a part
Of something greater than their daily toil
And poverty, and lack, had bred in them;
Of being somehow crowned
Themselves, as if on their heads too had poured
The benediction of the holy oil.

I wanted to re-charge the Church, not break it,
To clear the clutter and retain the core—
A Church well-organized as I could make it:
The English Bible now in every church,
And Cranmer's masterpiece of Common Prayer.

To reconcile God's purpose with man's reason
And, as Erasmus told us, "Not to narrow
What Christ meant to be broad". With Thomas More
I loved the church's form, but came to hate
The vices that obscured religion's marrow,
The covetous and tricky Roman State;
The drunken priests hauled out of every tavern,
Criminals, whom the church would re-instate
And judges might not sentence. Most of all
The hated mortuary, whereby the priest
Would claim the very garments of the dead,
Even the candles round about his head,
The fees for every sacrament; communion
For poor men dying, stopped for lack of pence—

Too much was there to anger and appal
But nothing lethal, in the Church's state:
Disease, not death, such matters indicate.

And yet, the Church has lost the way of heaven
When men can say, as said a priest of Devon—
"For if one can flatter, and wear a hawk on his fist
He shall be parson of Honiton or Clyst".
A Church for toadies, sporting gentlemen,
A church too smart,
Can hardly have Christ's matter at its heart
And needs re-making;
Needs a profound and catalystic shaking.

Heaven forfend that ever I should destroy
Faith that has been my lantern, man and boy.
Faith that has held the western world together,
From loved Byzantium, from fortress Rome,
In face of Huns, Moors, Turks, and stormy weather,
And failed Crusaders trailing wanly home.

Henry

Two Popes at once, indulgencies, false relics,
Infidel practises, and pagan joy,
Schism and anarchy, and Plague and fire,
The streets of Rome awash with innocent blood—
        No! simply to ***renew*** is my desire.

        As for the Pope, let him be Senior Bishop,
The ***Primus inter pares***,
        First among equals, Doyen of the Corps—
        But he can be no more;
Bound as he is by politics and pressure.

35

Henry

Yet noisy heresies assault my age
        And plaguey echoes answer,
Rousing in me an unforgiving rage.

Anne Askew, scarce a moment off the rack
Proclaims with her first breath
She never heard that Christ or his disciples
        Put anyone to death!
Lord, how these uninstructed women quack—

And these dim heresies, how they distress
An honest Catholic, who near his end
        Would like religious quiet!
Sir Thomas More, that good, mistaken friend
Who, too, believed in burning Protestants,
        Was also right in this—
Calling the bible in English ''filthiness''.
Reading it wrongly can provoke a riot.

''No woman, nor no common man should read it''
I have pronounced in no uncertain voice.
There'll be no end to the discrepancies
Twixt this and holy dogma they'll discover
        Given so wide a choice.

Without a doubt, Plato and Aristotle
And all the open-ness of free discussion
Have loosed an awkward genie from the bottle.

How strange that men rescued form distant dictats
        Of an infallible Pope
Will not accept law from my cleverer self
Good churchman now as any man alive—
        But still dispute and strive!

For a last time I gathered Parliament
On Christmas Eve of fifteen forty-five.
Archbishops and the Bishops, Lords and Commons;

Henry

For the last time behind respectful backs
I heard the great doors slam.

Heavy and shrewd, I listened to their address,
Then took a mighty breath—

"Of qualities and gifts
Barren and bare I am,
But thankful also to a merciful God
Who's given me such virtues, as you say
I have, 'incorporate within my person'.
Once again came the thanks, the pregnant pauses,
The 'trust they'd shown in voting me the money'
For charities, for colleges, good causes,
'More godly and more goodly than your will
Or your desire'. I told them of my care
For these good things (mellow as any honey)
Then, as they preened themselves with these fair words,
I showed them once again the basilisk stare,

A look malignant, and extremely bad
For nervous systems stretched to breaking point;
Some dreaded that I really had gone mad
Listening with fear intense,
And rapidly rejoicing
When I addressed them with such power and sense."

"No Prince of all the world more loves and favours
His subjects than I love and favour you
For whose defence my treasure is not hidden",
My very person jeopardized unbidden.

Eyes stared at me, as if to leave their heads.
They waited for the terrifying—"But . . .

All this may change:
Take pains to see this feeling stays the same.
One thing is far remiss and out of order—
Religious disputation has free range."

"Concord and charity are not among you"
I thundered out,
Strife and dissension rule in every place
Splitting of hairs is now the native game.
Is this the way to grace?

"What love and charity is this among you?"
Some will shout, Papist! some cry, Heretick!
As if abuse were any contribution.
"Some are too stiff in their old mumpsimus"
And will proceed no further with solution,
And many others
Are too high-handed with their elder brothers

Henry

"Busy and curious in new sumpsimus . . .
Amend these crimes, I straitly here exhort you . . .
Or, as God's vicar . . . I will surely see . . . "
Division made extinct, in a degree
That will most rudely sort you.

For the laymen here—
The Bible is not given as ammunition
That men should "rail and taunt against the clergy . . . "
I am ashamed to hear
How "that most precious jewel, the word of God",
That should be doubly dear
"Is jangled, rhymed, disputed in alehouses".
Use it to teach your young; and all aspire
To love, to serve, to dread Almighty God,
And this, as Sovereign Lord, I most require.

Amidst a total hush, my ending came:
And with a kind of wonder, a still awe,
They all received the same;
Amazed to see
This vibrant and continued potency.

As innocent of humbug as a lamb
I stood and savoured this my splendid hour—
Final exertion of authority
On those who all accept me as I am—
A glowing conscience, with a line direct
To the Almighty God.

I heard my voice resound
Ringing, direct, and potent as a flame.

Words are not vitiated, though the ground
From which they come is not devoid of blame;
No! nor in issuing forth from my grotesque
And nearly dying frame.

How tepid life must be, how soft and tame,
With no more such an hour,
Without the strong intoxicant of power!

* * * *

Henry

Now, at length, ended one prolonged romance,
In a great treaty that renounced Boulogne,
(Accepting feudal dues for it instead),
I rendered up my lifelong claim to France.

To my son Edward, I bequeathed alone
The imperial crown of England, and her throne
As well of Ireland, "Without title to France . . . "

Henry

Ah, those brave acres of Anjou and Maine,
Castles, and orchards and deep Norman pastures
          My fathers once did own!
That long-desired and rich inheritance.

Berry, Orléans, and Touraine well cropped,
The sunny vinyards south in Aquitaine
So long and bravely fought for! and released
With hardy realism, but with pain—
          A strong limb lopped.

*   *   *   *

Henry

Men still cry 'Bluebeard' at me, and play darts
With my six wives, as if they were six puppets,
          Or six hilarious stories.
Sex is a glory; there are other glories;
Life was not centred in my private parts.
I was as happy hunting, or at sea,
          With a strong bow, to shoot,
Or riding at the head of armoured men,
Or making music with the pleading lute—
Master of all the best of pleasure's arts.

36

Henry

I could still terrify and even tease;
          And often did.
No machinations were completely hid
By which men sought to push advantages.
Cranmer was summoned now for heresy
By Gostewycke, who was Bedfordshire's M.P.
And presently, by Gardiner, to the Council.

I cried to gentle Cranmer, "O Lord God!
          What fond simplicity have you
So to permit yourself to be imprisoned . . .
Do not you think, that once you are in prison,
Three or four false knaves soon will be procured
That dare not open lips before your face"
(There's never been a scarcity of them),
"To witness bear against you and to condemn?"

          I rescued him, of course,
          And let his sly accusers
Feel fury breaking on them like a storm.
          "How have you handled here
My Lord of Canterbury?" I asked the Council,
          Trembling to hear me then,
—Cold hearts, but brows with sweat grown deadly warm—

Henry

"Shutting him from the Council Chamber,
Made to wait
Among the serving men?
Would you be handled so yourselves:
At someone else's hand?
"You should well understand
I count my Lord as faithful towards me
As ever there was prelate in this realm."
And after that durst never a fellow spurn him
Whilst I was at the helm.

I argued still with Cranmer, whom I called
"The greatest heretic in all of Kent",
Half jokingly, and half sincerely meant.
Who knows but in our lengthy disputations
We should have come together
Granted a longer span;
I gave him leave to educate my son.

"And what is this" I asked him "that we pray
And lead us not into temptation?"
Surely this ought to be, I said
"Suffer us not to be led?"
Cranmer replied "Christ taught us thus to pray".
I loved him for his gracefulness of tongue
And for his total absence of ambition,
I loved him, and I let him have his way.

And yet not always, as we sat and argued.
—Cyprian, Origen, Isaiah, Proverbs—
So up and down, and to and fro we went
Discourse and learning in our friendship blent.
And yet I feared the gentleness, and the assent
He bore too much to royalty, knowing not
Who might in time succeed me.
"What will they do to you when I am gone?"
I asked, prophetic of men's ill intent,
And of those bitter flames.

"Surely I reckon that you will tell the truth,
Yea, of yourself, so be you have offended?"
Without my strong abrasive certainties
Where might his fairness and his balance lead him?
Here was one friendship that was never ended.

Nervous, unsure, from that schoolmaster bully
Who daunted him in childhood, he was yet
One who could draw the heartstrings, who could fully
Summon his music from the mysterious air
With every sentence set
In the long lilt and cadence of his words;
Who could transform the very stuff of dogma
Charming us with the sweetness of this pulley.

Henry

All the uneducated, and the dim
For full four hundred years
Could understand him perfectly; but these
More dim successors in his noble see,
Can but decree
Now that the flock entire is educated,
That Cranmer has become too difficult
For these bright folk to see,
And so he has to be
Replaced by journalese.

Cranmer, my pliant and long-lasting friend—
The daunted man who made a dauntless end.

* * * *

Henry

People still cheered me as I rode about
Cruel though I was, and now extremely gross.
For what dies last in personality,
Buried however deep, is native charm—
A curious gold that never turns to dross.

Suffolk, my hunting crony, had now died,
But Catherine loved me, or perhaps she did.
And there was my poor fool, and several others
Still unafraid, who treated me like brothers.

I never cared for argument at table,
That is a place to eat, and to be jolly
With laughter and with wine.
Theology, at home,
Makes a man long to roam.

But Catherine, the clever, loved such talk.
I beg you, I would tell her, let it be.
(A woman arguing,
With insufficient intellectual basis
Has always been anathema to me);
Though Catherine, to be fair
In her discourse was gentle, almost tame,
Had no contentious air.
But to ambitious courtiers
Religious questions made her easy game.

These made a thrust to implicate poor Catherine
My last, intelligent, pacific wife.
Norfolk and Bishop Gardiner, they attacked
Through Mrs Askew, whom they apprehended
And had her racked.
An arrogant, wild lady, who once said
"What do you call your God? A piece of bread?"
Naturally, we burnt her; but half dead

Henry

She implicated no-one; by her silence
Queen Catherine, who once heard her, was defended.

A nagging doubt still harboured in my breast.
"Much to my comfort is it in mine age
To be taught clerkly matters by my wife",
I furiously said, one day when Catherine
Spoke godliness with me, at an ill moment.
And so I agreed
When Bishop Gardiner proposed arrest.

Always the peaceable, she did not argue,
But gently wept, bending a fair face down.
(Gentleness, surely, is a woman's crown,
How I once loved the gentleness of Jane!)
Then told me she had spoken but to please,
To pass the time and ease me of my pain—
My now devouring, devilish, constant pain.

Suddenly, I became myself again,
To Norfolk's schemes alerted
And so held out my hand to peaceful Catherine;
A horrible injustice was averted.

"Ye are become a doctor, Kate, to teach us?"
I roared, in kindly chaff.
Quietly she said, "no, but I hoped to learn".
"Is it so, sweetheart? . . . We are friends again"
I said, with my great laugh.
All was now ease and pardon,
We went to walk together in the garden.

So when they came with pikemen to arrest her
I turned on them, an angry lion at bay,
Bade them begone, called Wriothesley a knave,
Would have arrested him, till gentle Catherine
Who always was most merciful to save,
And kindly to my children, pleaded for him.

"You little know" I said
"How evil he deserves grace at your hands".
Poor Chancellor, he crept aghast away;
For he and Norfolk now had had their day.
But from the old Church I was not to sever,
I followed still her ritual faithfully,
Every Good Friday my old stubborn limbs
Still wearily went creeping to the Cross.
Heretics burned as merrily as ever,
I called on every saint,
And never let my long devotions faint.
Abbeys might suffer loss,
But schools and colleges increased as never.

Henry

I sought to make provision for the poor
Whom once the monks had aided, and my law
Left them, I thought, much better than before.
Even my fierceness, now and then would break,
The poet Blage, condemned for heresy.
My intervention rescued from the stake.

Reader

Condemned to death, and certain of his fate
Blage wrote an apologia for his life,
In protest at the priests who took men's bibles
And cast them on the fire
Leaving the luckless owners desolate.

Blage

. . . "Our guides have erred and walked out of the way
And we by them full craftily are trapped,
Whom they should lead, they drive out of array.
The living word, the bread of life from us
By mighty hand extorted have these men
Feigning as though it were food dangerous,
And for God's wheat, feed us with Bishop's bren,[1]
Thus do they sift the chaff from the good corn,
The bad they keep, the best throw out of door
Their simple flock thus so they mock and scorn . . .

Hold over us, O Lord, thy holy hand . . .
Weigh not our works nor look not to our deeds
Thy mercy pure upon us down distil,
They seem fair flowers that in thy sight are weeds
Without thy grace nought can we do but ill . . .

And I O Lord into thy hands do yield
My faithful soul, appointed now of thee
This life to leave thorough fire in Smithfield
By which I shall be rid of misery . . .

To thee O Christ which in the heaven on high
By the Father on the right hand doth sit
My sinful soul to thee Lord I commit
Assured well that saved it shall be
For no deserts but of thy mere mercy . . ."

Reader

What tipped the scales in favour of George Blage?
Probably not this hasty written page.
It is unlikely that the King saw these
Or felt their poignancy,
But George Blage was set free
Henry won't have him scuppered with the rest.

Some other Protestants were not so blest.

[1] bran

Henry

For, fully Catholic in my intent,
I burned a man for eating meat in Lent.

No celibate myself, I still insisted
On celibacy for the hapless priest.

I still believed in transubstantiation,
Holding to four old sacraments at least.

Yet, as pure Catholic, I came to falter;
In certain forms I ceased to celebrate,
In some ideas I would not tolerate.
As I grew older I rejected creeping
On abject knees from the church door to altar;
        God is, for sure,
        No eastern potentate
Insisting men should grovel at his feet:
This is but self-inflicted punishment
        That certain souls find sweet.
Hair-shirts, prostrations, Romish practises
Became for me no longer right and meet.

        Constant with praise and prayer,
Deeply convinced that God is really there;
Though arguing with churchmen to the last
        I breathed a free-er air;

        Still failing to translate
My faith into my actions, or relate
My deeds of unequivocal self-will
To precepts I continued to instill
        —With ruthless certainty—
Into the listening subjects of my state.

Reader

        The mystery of it all
Lies in long years when they refused to hate;
        The habit of affection,
        Taking its old direction,
Rising above a conduct to appal.

37

Henry

The pain within my ulcerated leg
        Lasted eleven years.
Tormenting me increasingly; and so
        Grievances grow,
And temper, still extravagant and rash.
        Syphilis? Surely, No!
Such news would have to go
Round Western Europe in a lightning flash
Delighting enemies. It never did.

Reader

This ***canard*** has been lately put about
By keen historians seeking something new;
Contemporaries never mention it.
The pain he suffered so continually
Was nothing more sensational than gout.
He paid the penalty for over-eating
He was as full of protein as an egg;
What killed him was blood pressure
And an occluded sinus in his leg.

Henry

So all this pain and power,
Was totally corrupting all the while;
Though never tiring me or my quick brain
As yearly I grew larger and more vile.

A certain clarity abode within.
A settled iron logic drove me on,
Whose purpose was, so to protect my son
So shortly to be left, and not yet ten,
—My sparky son—against malicious men,
So that no subtle force should overwhelm him
And set the realm to ruin. Was this sin?
In this betraying epoch, who could tell
Where a corrupt ambition lurked within?

It was for this I butchered Poles and Courtenays,
And Buckingham, long since,
For Royal blood they never could forget
The burning blazon of Plantagenet.

Reader

Now, brilliant, rash, poetic Surrey fell—
This potent royal myth
Had captured, too, his bright imagination
And sounded, soon, his knell.

Henry

A kind of love directed all this hate,
For England, for my son, for the brave past
For which I sought hopeful continuance,
Whose glories I desired to emulate
And deadly dangers to anticipate,
Striking, as ever, to the very heart;
Just as a most peculiar love of God
Dictated all religious persecutions
On either side;
Directing those revolting executions.

My purpose and my brain did not depart,
I rode and hunted almost to the last
Persistent in my pleasure-seeking pride.
I read the whole of Surrey's trial through,
Noting the arguments, and making comments
The day before I died.

He had proclaimed his case with force and spirit—
Surrey "Henry of Surrey never yet
For profit was corrupted,
Nor ever yet did bribery close his hand".
Henry Rash fellow! He could never understand
My fear that his proud blood had interrupted
Or could, my son's smooth passage to the throne.

My final legal murder here was done.
In these last days the young and gallant Surrey
Died of his arrogance, who might have thrived,
A poet fine enough. But too vainglorious—
He bore the arms on his heraldic shield
Proper to Edward, Prince of Wales, alone—
A gaffe notorious.

"And what importeth this?" I asked the jury,
A bold bid for the throne?
Reader So fell the axe on Surrey, while his father
Old crafty Norfolk, in the Tower, attainted,
Waited, and so survived.

* * * *

Henry By Christmas I had understood my state
And sent for daughter Mary, with regret
Her life had not a happier tale to tell.
"Fortune hath been against thee, and I grieve
Not to have had thee married as I wished . . .
Look to thy brother, he is little yet"
I told her. And her deep voice, solemn, stricken,
Full of her mother's Spanish melancholy,
Uttered a pious, dutiful farewell.
Forgiveness? Love? Or wrath? In that close soul
Who knows? Who now can tell?

Reader Elizabeth and Edward were not there
To see death's face; but at the final news,
Though children, surely, cannot weep to order,
Their two red heads went down
And they wept sorely at a world left bare.

Henry Late January, I made annuities
For all my servants, and for Catherine
Most generously; commanded men to treat her
As when I lived; and organized a Council
With Hertford (Edward Seymour) at its head,
Judging he would be faithful to his nephew
Reader (As he proved to be)
Henry Long after I was dead.

Henry When one brave courtier told me
That I was like to die, I never faltered,
Confident now as I had ever been.
Personal fear was never yet my devil—
Nor did the final terror leave me altered.

Reader He was the strong man armed, who kept his palace;
The stronger one he knew not, who should come
And should divide the spoils;
Or knowing him, forgot
In the exultant splendour of his lot.

Henry Now, gross and failing, I will still defy him
The lordly and inexorable death—
Live while I may, and exercise my will,
Defy his puissance, struggle in his toils.
Whatever waits, there's no more majesty
—Or none for me—
''Stronger than he!''
But while I breathe I reign,
Let this strong adversary show his banner,
I'll guard my citadel in my own manner.

Reader The end came swiftly (undeservedly,
It might be said).
Defeated doctors round about his bed.

What thoughts infect the minds of dying men
The virtuous, the bad, the mediocre?
They do not tell us. In our game of cards
Death is the final joker.
And he is played superbly, now and then.

Henry Reality and dreams . . .
They mingle now within the spinning head . . .
Shadowy faces hover, voices come
As from some valley infinitely far
And hollow, and forsaken of its streams.

The dry hands rasp along the silken sheet,
Plucking, forever plucking . . .
Men moved about me, silent and discreet.

My long tumultuous life gathered around me
Seeming to me fragmented and frustrated,
Nothing accomplished, nothing left complete . . .

Prophetic sadness seeming to blot out
All that was lovely, all remembrance sweet . . .

Some wanton devils all my hopes destroy—
Edward the King, my dear son, died a boy,

Henry

My promising, my longed-for, killed-for, son,
Neglected and outworn by powerful men,
Though he might well have proved
As forceful and uncaring as myself,
At twelve, already he defied the Emperor.
Mary was childless, Bess would never marry,
None of them were to bring a child to birth,
        Most were not long to tarry;
None of my getting walk the happy earth.
Even my bastard son, the handsome Richmond
        Whose dear companionship
Shines ever in the poetry of Surrey,
Died also, childless, early, of consumption.
        I've no continuance
In this great realm my subtlety and skill
Mastered and strengthened, that they might enjoy.
        My children all, are still.
        And sister Margaret's this long wealth employ.

Reader

Never despair; and never be afraid
For the completion of man's noble ends.
        God may in time fulfil
Our best ambition in another manner
Than that our narrow calculation made.
The burning purpose never will be laid,
        However long delayed.
For when our strenuous hearts at length are still
        Great purposes unfold
In ways unthought by us, forms unforetold,
        Wrought by his holy will,
When winter storms bring in an age of gold.

Henry

Young Edward founded schools that long endure,
And even Mary's cruel persecutions
Contrariwise, made England more secure—
At one against the Catholics and Spain.
While great Elizabeth, my slighted daughter,
With all my red-haired rogue tenacity,
Child of my wilfulness, and also child
Of dark-haired Anne, my spirit's deepest bane,
        Ruled not in vain,
        Kept to my dearest cause;
Held all together through the dangerous rage
Of an indignant Europe, made the land
Secure from any more dynastic wars—
A country that had truly come of age.

While France and Holland, Germany, Bohemia
Drown in a sea of calumny and blood,
Where Christians butcher Christians in God's name
For Thirty Years, in savagery's full flood,
Elizabeth these passions will bewail,

Queen Elizabeth — Seeking for "windows into no man's soul",
And longing for the deep wounds to be whole.

Reader — She persecuted none, until the Pope
Calling upon her subjects to dethrone her
        Dowsed that mild hope.

Queen Elizabeth — "There is but one Christ Jesus, and one faith,
The rest is disputation over trifles",
She said; and after many bitter years
This truth at length would blossom and prevail.

Reader — The hands continued plucking, ever moving,
        Swift dissolution proving.

Henry — My great idea—settled, United Kingdom
Living within its equitable laws—
        Will not for long have pause.
Though not perhaps exactly as we planned
        I and my daughter Bess
Between us, left you an unbreakable land.

Also my ships, my ships and their successors,
My ships at sea, would carry Magna Carta,
Habeas Corpus, and the rule of Law,
And trial by jury, and an equal justice
        To the most distant shore,
        Under my flag unfurled.
The English Bible, Cranmer's Common Prayer,
And Shakespeare's glories that are yet unwritten,
My undefeated ships will proudly bear
To outposts of the undiscovered world.

These were my children, these my great-grandchildren—
        The hardy ships-of-the-line,
Revenge, and Resolution, Royal Sovereign,
Renown, and Royal Oak, and Ramillies,
Unwearied, and undaunted, like a sign
        Of human hope unshaken;
Climbing the savage seas, smooth oceans carving,
To scatter foes, and succour the forsaken;
Waves curling from them into foaming fern;
        At every rounded stern
The red cross of St George's flag unfurled,
        The constant ships-of-the-line
        Who, once or twice, saved Europe,
        And once or twice, the world.

Reader — However cruel, however little meant,
Wicked King Henry was the instrument
        Of much we now enjoy—

Reader

Free speaking and free writing, without tears,
That no-one else in Europe could employ
For several hundred years.

38

Reader

A January night;
The King is dying . . .
On tower and wall the weary sentinels
Keep their grim watch,
Guard what is now past guarding.
Only recurrent bells
—Sounds that deride the sleepless and the sad—
Break the long spells
Of passing . . . passing . . . ever passing time.
Can Henry hear them yet? Their studious chime
Echoes and emphasizes
The steady movement of our mortal river
Towards that sea where moons no more decline,
And no sun rises.

Men gathered in the icy winter dusk.
A silent night was slowly, brightly starred . . .
Fingers of frost reached downward through the earth
To kill, and to prepare.
Apothecary voices, scent of musk
Hung on the crowded air,
Faintly was heard the stamping of the guard . . .
Flames of the fire leapt upwards, as in mirth,
Courtiers in velvet doublets came and went,
Jewel-coloured, jewel-hard.

Henry

They gazed with avid eyes
To garner all the horror they could glean.
A kind of grim surmise
Lit eyes that once were lowered to combine
Humility with pride;
Eyes narrow and as merciless as mine,
From love or pity free.
The death of absolute power
For lesser men is wonderful to see.

And yet they trembled still to look on me
Hiding their exultation with long faces,
For while I yet had breath
My terrible lips could utter life or death
Even at this last hour
For friends condemned and waiting in the Tower.

The stream of faith still murmured and outpoured
Within my failing flesh.

Henry

"Mercy of Christ could pardon all my sins"
I said, "though they were greater than they be".
  My will was still as strong
  However limbs grew weak;
Asked of a priest, I answered "Only Cranmer,
And he not yet". I took a little sleep.
And yet too long; waking, I could not speak.

Cranmer the faithful, and a man apart
Within the genious of his liturgies—
Stayed by me with his holy consolation
Before my giant frame destroyed my heart;
Though I could only signify repentance
And my belief in Christ's redemptive love
By an agreeing pressure on the hand
Of this uncertain and forgiving man
My old Archbishop.
    He could understand,
Comfort, and pray within my speechless lips
  At this, my dread eclipse.

  Only his voice I heard
In infinite remoteness, and yet near,
Asking if I repented and believed.
Through the thick fog of imminent death it sounded,
  Unseen, but clear.

  The absolute enduringness of God
Came strongly through it, and the sword of Christ
  Pierced my hard heart
  As breath came faint and shallow.

Still the cold pressure of my dying hand
On Cranmer's clasp was answered surely by him,
  And my harsh soul, relieved
Of hatred and of fear, of pain's confusion,
Of weakness and its dread ally, despair,
  Of clouding, dark suspicion—
  By this one human hand
Was sped with blessing into the unknown land.

As at the end of some prodigious storm
  The red sun fiercely setting
With brilliant, level rays, the scene illumes,
While the torn clouds drift slowly into shape
Their rugged wild incontinence forgetting,
  And their calm form resumes,
So did my soul, for whom the demons gape
Shake off my ill and disobedient flesh
  And pass to rest,
  Cranmer's kind hand abetting.

* * * *

Reader

So ended Henry, by the Grace of God,
The King of England, Ireland and of France,
Defender of the Faith, the King of Scotland,
And Prince of mountained Wales.
Here ends the lordly span;
And mighty majesty no more prevails.
Here begins Henry, spent departing soul,
Naked as any other mortal man.

His huge unwieldly corpse
Free at long last of pain
Lowered uneasily into the vault
Within St George's Church, at Windsor Castle.
And by his will, is buried close beside
His most beloved, Queen Jane.

* * * *

Reader

The heartless and triumphant trumpets ring
Proclaiming Edward, by the Grace of God
Of England, and his full dominions, King,
Successor without question to the throne.

And two young red-haired children weep alone.

Boy's voice singing contemporary song

"Sing up heart, sing up heart,
And sing no more down,
But joy in King Edward
That weareth the Crown."

Choir repeating

* * * *

Reader

Long long ago, beside a bluer sea
Than ever around England may be seen,
By stonier hills, far from her magic green,
Some pessimistic persons out of Corinth
Listened without conviction to Saint Paul.

Judge no-one, he besought, before the time.
When everything about a man is known
No single motive left obscure at all,
—The far-spread evil and the puny good—
Down every pathway of the route he trod;
When light illuminates

St Paul

"The hidden darkness . . .
The counsels of the heart made manifest"
Long buried sin confessed,

Reader

Then, only then shall all be understood,

St Paul

"And then shall every man have praise of God".